MW00895602

If I Was God

GERRY BAST

A FRESH LOOK
AT SOME VERY OLD IDEAS

 **FriesenPress**

Suite 300 - 990 Fort St
Victoria, BC, Canada, V8V 3K2
www.friesenpress.com

Copyright © 2015 by Gerry Bast
First Edition — 2015

All rights reserved.

No part of this publication may be reproduced in any form, or by any means, electronic or mechanical, including photocopying, recording, or any information browsing, storage, or retrieval system, without permission in writing from the publisher.

ISBN
978-1-4602-2127-3 (Hardcover)
978-1-4602-2126-6 (Paperback)
978-1-4602-2128-0 (eBook)

1. Religion, Faith

Distributed to the trade by The Ingram Book Company

Cover Art graciously provided by Dan Murphy, Calgary, Alberta.

DEDICATION

—

To my parents,
Mahlon and Norma Bast,
who, though they tried,
could never think inside the box.

Table of Contents

Is the Universe Friendly?

INTRODUCTION

Life is filled with paradox.
Peace and conflict coexist.
Inner turmoil on one hand.
On the other, tranquillity.
Beauty surrounds us.
Tragedy fills the daily news.
Hope vs. despair.
Success or failure?
Love and hatred.
Excess and poverty.

Why are we so fragile?
Why does life have to be so hard?
How can joy and sorrow be such close neighbours?

If There Is a God, if there really is . . .
Then we must have all kinds of questions for her, mustn't we?

If There Was a God . . . planning, creating, and building when all the worlds were forming,

What did he really have in mind for this magnificent, terrifying, undiscoverable universe?

If There Is a God . . . out there right now, what the heck are we supposed to do?
Is this God hiding from us?

Are we all required to go through religious ceremony in order to make contact?

If I Was God . . . what would I have done?
Would I have created something similar?
Would I have taken the risk of placing sentient beings in such a danger-filled world?

Think about it—our hearts are easily broken.
Emotions flare up without our consent and beyond our control.
The human mind breaks down. Bones fracture.
Muscles bruise and tear.

What about our stomachs, intestinal ailments, bone disease, and joint pain?
The expanding knowledge base of dis-ease seems endless.
And yet, if we admit it, we realize that our most common "sins" spring from an over-indulgence in life's free gifts of pleasure.

What is it all about?

These questions have been asked by our most renowned philosophers down through the ages.

I am no scholar, and I know that only a fool would try to write a book that promises answers to all of the pressing questions facing humanity.

However, I ask myself . . . If I Was God, could I have made a better world for us to dwell in?

And seriously, if there is a God,
Is this the best she can do?

C S Lewis, author of *The Chronicles of Narnia* and *Mere Christianity*, commented on how humans have been endowed with an ability to suffer in a way that animals cannot. It goes something like this:

1. We have the unique capacity to ache in anticipation as we look forward with fear toward an impending future event.

2. When the situation finally arrives, we feel every ounce of its agony.

3. After the event is past, we can also look back and relive it a third time.

We experience painful memories day after day, year after year. Should I mention the heartache that comes from the common attack of guilt? And regret? What about those who are plagued with loneliness?

In the midst of all this, we have to ask why. What is the point? We are forced to wonder if there is anyone who hears us. Is there someone outside our realm of existence who is responsible? We are tempted to take Oscar Wilde seriously when he said "I think God, in creating man, somewhat overestimated his ability."

Perhaps our thoughts betray a secret fear: "Maybe this is only an experiment. You know, maybe somebody is watching, but only to see how we react."

If life as we know it is a test, the stakes are very high.

We can sink so low. Then without warning, and by no apparent effort on our part, we magically break through into a season of joy. New relationships unfold. Friendships form. Maybe success knocks on our door or we fall in love. Young couples and not-so-young alike find companionship. Together they commit "to have and to hold for as long as we both shall live."

Stop for just a moment and look into the eyes of a child who, in innocence, cannot conceal the wonder of everyday life. So much beauty exists all around us. Acts of kindness reveal the depth and value in being human.

Consider planet Earth. How can we even begin to explain the gift we call home?

I have driven as far as the road allowed and then hiked to the top of a mountain. We looked westward over the rugged peaks of the Rocky Mountains in Kananaskis Country, south of Banff, Alberta. A hawk soared high above the trees . . . hundreds of feet below us. Down in an open field a herd of wild elk grazed.

Photo by Jill and Gerry Bast

On top of that very mountain the soil was largely gravel. We looked in awe at the plants thriving in the cold, thin atmosphere. Nothing grew taller than a few inches in height. Covering much of the desert-like area, where humans rarely attend, tiny flowers with intricate design and vibrant colour seemed to cry out, "Look at me!"

Photo by Jill and Gerry Bast

We have peered through the branches of an ancient rainforest in British Columbia to find a pristine stream flowing gently downward beside wildflowers and oversized ferns. Moss draped itself over vines spanning the trees.

Photo by Jill and Gerry Bast

My wife, Jill, and I watched a couple of very large bears feasting on roots and vegetation across a valley. We wondered at his fate as a lone Rocky Mountain sheep walked up the hill in the bears' direction. We could see it all unfold. Finally, a small cluster of trees was the only thing that separated the little guy from these two beasts. As he broke through the brush and stumbled upon them, he made an abrupt about-face and a much quicker descent than his lazy climb had been. I don't know if the giant teddies even turned around, but he didn't wait to find out.

We have had the good fortune to encounter several bears on our wilderness experiences . . . from a safe distance, of course. We sense the assurance of belonging when nature comes out to greet us.

This guy posed for us on the side of the road.

Photo by Jill and Gerry Bast

Along that same highway we stopped to marvel at mountain peaks that never look the same as the last time we drove through. Nor do they reveal themselves as they had only two hours earlier. Moment by moment, the angle of the sun illumines anew in the endless spectrum of colour.

Photo by Gerry and Jill Bast

Returning from a holiday to British Columbia, just before the Alberta border we had to stop and capture this majestic elk grazing beside the road.

Photo by Jill and Gerry Bast

Before we even had time to catch our breath, we rounded a corner and the landscape of the Rocky Mountains lay before us.

Photo by Jill and Gerry Bast

Life is good in so many ways. When my "kids" come over for family dinner (eighteen of them last time) the conversation amplifies with a strange excitement. The decibels rise and laughter rings out—you would think we were at a bar trying to outshout a live band! I smile from deep within. Beautiful, crazy, lovable human beings!

We are all afforded these moments of exhilaration! Months and even years filled with hope may creep up on us. Lifelong friends enrich us. And yet, just down the street and across the ocean, catastrophe beyond our imagination tears at the very fabric of someone else's existence.

The challenge of this literary/photographic/interactive offering will be to find the proper "voke." That's right, the proper voke.

I will be on my guard to make sure that I do not attempt only to PRO-voke.

Some provocation must occur. However, if I make that my sole purpose, then I fail before I begin.

I also hope to IN-voke the gods to give us wisdom. Could some ideas serve as a serious invocation and call forth a passionate response from you, the reader? If so, accept it as inspiration.

And I will endeavour to E-voke! I will choose to evoke questions, deeper consideration, and open-minded discussion about the wild world we inhabit. Through the questions we will ask, and because of the world we have been gifted with, I will attempt to bring readers to a picture of God that can be embraced without fear. My goal is your renewed faith.

So as you are reading, if you find yourself rethinking, asking questions, and taking a second look, then I will have succeeded. Let me thank you in advance, then, for at least taking a first look at *If I Was God*.[1]

---

1   For updates and to view all photos in full color please go to www.ifiwasgod.ca

CHAPTER 1

A Look at Nature

Nature is brimming with wonder. Complexity and intricate design are so common we take them for granted. And beauty now bores us.

I raised my glass of full bodied, Argentinian Malbec red wine and said, "If I was God, I would make you."

Someone congratulated me. "Hey. That's good enough to be the title of a CD."

I thought, "If you only knew. It's the title and theme of a book I hope to get published some day."

Some eighteen people were scattered throughout the living/dining area of our home. A great meal was ready to be served. It was Easter and we were having "Family Dinner."

Jill and I, our two kids, their significant others, and some kids we had unofficially adopted over the years rose to find food and a place to sit. One of the fifty-somethings was a father with his twenty-something son. There was a couple with a newborn. Another pair with two kids was unavailable. We were graced by the presence of our beautiful girl from France, who now could say she had family here in Calgary. We had fallen in love with all of them over the years and selfishly claimed them as our own. My heart soared as I shared a meal with this motley assortment of amazing creatures. Is there any animal as beautiful as the human? Is there anything in nature as complex?

So now I am looking through a dictionary. How far do I have to go to find a specimen from the animal kingdom that also makes me stop and wonder? Immediately I find a word that starts with the letters "Aa." Let's consider the aardvark, shall we?

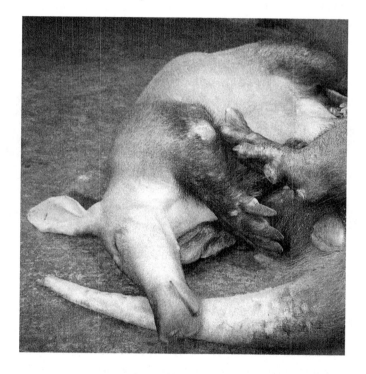

This is a photo of a resting aardvark at the Himeji City Zoo, Japan.

(After hours of searching I could not find the name of the author of this file to give proper attribution. See http://commons.wikimedia.org/wiki/User:Opencage

Perhaps the name was right in front of me, plainly stated in, what is, to my uneducated eyes, a maze of Japanese symbols. You can see all the photos offered by following the links.)

http://upload.wikimedia.org/wikipedia/commons/e/ee/Orycteropus_afer.jpg

Aardvarks look like somebody took parts from several animals and attached them to the body of a bear or a pig. A long tubular snout similar to the anteater and donkey's ears makes them much more than unique. They are the one and only living representative of the Tubulidentata (tube-toothed). Which means there is really nothing else like the aardvark. With spoon-shaped claws, tubular teeth and snout, and sticky foot-long tongues, one aardvark can eat fifty-thousand insects in a single day.

http://en.wikipedia.org/wiki/Anteater

Giant Anteater by Danish photographer Malene Thyssen. http://commons. wikimedia.org/wiki/User:Malene

You might think these two guys are the same, but the Anteater has no teeth and no long tongue. Who needs teeth when you can grind food up in your stomach with the help of the sand you've just swallowed? He is just about twice the size of the aardvark, yet weighs only half as much. Up to seven feet long, anteaters live above ground and don't burrow like the aardvark.

Sandwiched between aardvark and anteater in my dictionary is the most industrious little creature: the ant. An unfortunate placement. In the end, the lion may lie down with the lamb, but how will this tiny creature relax beside these two? Think for a moment about this common insect that, under normal circumstances, is just an annoyance.

Thomas Endlein www.antark.net/ant-facts/#.UzeAScIrTTZ then click on ant fact #2

Used by Permission

1. Some ants can carry one-hundred times their weight while hanging upside down ON GLASS!

2. "This photo of an Asian Weaver Ant carrying a weight while using the sticky pads on its feet to walk upside down won the Biotechnology and Biological Sciences Research Council Photography prize." (Thomas Endlein, University of Cambridge)

3. Ants can live longer than any other insect. One queen was recorded to have lived for thirty years.

4. There are more than twelve-thousand known species of ants.

5. The total weight of ants in the world is close to or even greater than that of all humans.

Photo by Andrea Izzotti. See www.fotolia.com/

It looks to me as though some of the DNA from the armadillo was integrated with a squirrel. That is some cool armour!

Check out a cute website called DIVaboo for the 25 World's Weirdest Animals.

Strangely, humans aren't listed in the top 25!

"We mention nature and forget ourselves in it: we ourselves are nature, quand meme. As a result, nature is something entirely different from what comes to mind when we invoke its name."
-Friedrich Niestzsche

Also in the list of the 25 Weirdest Animals is the Axolotl. Just a glance at this little creature expands our picture of the vast array of creativity displayed in the animal kingdom.

Photo credit Maslov Dmitry. See his portfolio at www.shutterstock.com/g/argument

And then there is the Aye-Aye from Madagascar. Someone once manipulated photos to place an Aye-Aye onto the shoulder of Marty Feldman. They say Marty took first place for the entry in Celebrity Pet Lookalikes.

Go to http://www.worth1000.com/ contests/20645/celebrity-pet-lookalikes

http://en.wikipedia.org/wiki/File:Aye-aye_at_night_in_the_wild_in_Madagascar. jpg

Photo by Frank Vassen.

We live in a crazy world, don't we? This short foray into the unusual in the animal kingdom was quick and easy to find, and we haven't even reached the letter "B." Shall we move on?

Go online and find the Blobfish. (I'm sorry but I couldn't find a usable photograph.) Its flesh is a gelatinous mass just less dense than that of water. Very pretty! Thus it floats just above the sea floor, at levels where the water pressure is dozens of times greater than at sea level. Under that pressure, its relative lack of muscle is not a disadvantage. Rather it is a means of survival. It bobs about, without muscle and bones to be crushed, and eats stuff that happens to swim just in front of it.

I had never heard of the Proboscis Monkey. This creature is also a work of art.

Photo by Frank Wouters – Antwerpen Belgium

http://en.wikipedia.org/wiki/Proboscis_monkey#mediaviewer/File:Proboscis_Monkey.jpg

Calgary photographer – Amy Asbury – was holidaying in Tofino, British Columbia when this little creature crawled up out of the Pacific Ocean. Thousands can be found every day. And they are edible. Food is climbing up out of the ocean for your dining pleasure.

Photo copyright Amy Asbury – www.amyasbury.ca

How many different kinds of animals are there in the world? The numbers cannot be discovered. Variety hardly expresses the magnitude of creativity. Countless species of fish, plankton, and microscopic sea creatures are just now being researched.

Here are some results from research done recently by the Census of Marine Life. *More than one million species* likely inhabit our oceans. Less than a quarter are described by science, and that's not counting microbes, which potentially number in the hundreds of millions.

Six thousand possible new marine species were added to the catalogue of life on Earth. *Formal scientific descriptions* were made of more than twelve-hundred new species. *Thirty-five thousand species* were barcoded (genetically analysed) in an effort that has redrawn our understanding of the tree of life.

Rare species turn out to be common in marine habitats.

However, even after a decade of intensive effort, the Census Database has no record for a large percentage of the ocean's volume.

Check out National Geographic - Hard-to-See Sea Creatures Revealed

Census of Marine Life www.coml.org

Image credit: Cheryl Clarke-Hopcroft/UAF/CMarZ

What a world we live in! Imagine a trillion of these guys (girls?) swimming together. This planet is teeming with life, with insects and seemingly purposeless creatures. Bats represent about twenty percent of all classified mammal species worldwide. About seventy percent are insectivores. Each one can eat 500 - 1000 mosquitoes in a single night. How many mosquitoes must there be? What are the insects here for? They feed bats and anteaters. Is that it? No. They are also servants of the plant world, carrying pollen from one plant to another. And they are obviously out for my blood.

Did you know that a cubic metre of soil can house one-thousand species of bugs and worms? One-thousand species of bugs digging, stirring, and fertilizing the soil.

Oh, this little black marble that we inhabit. It seems to dangle from a string amidst a sky full of ornaments.

More photos are available at http://www.petapixel.com/2012/12/05/
black-marble-nasa-releases-incredibly-detailed-photos-of-earth-at-night/

19

Go to http://en.wikipedia.org/wiki/Mars and follow the links. Half a billion people a month use Wikipedia. So much at our fingertips there and at a host of other web sites! We cannot and we must not hold to our old worldview any longer.

We now have real photos of Mars. Not so long ago we could only imagine what it must look like.

Below is my own photo of the moon; that celestial rock that just keeps dancing around Mother Earth day after day, year after year.

Photo by Gerry and Jill Bast

Tell me, do you have any idea how big this little cluster is?

European Southern Observatory. Photo credit Bruno Gilli
http://www.eso.org/public/images/milkyway/

Our galaxy is only one of hundreds of billions of galaxies, each of which has hundreds of billions of stars/suns. And we know there is more out there than we can discover.

What would persuade the Starter-Of-All-Of-This to actually . . . start all of this?

Is there a purpose for the boundless variety?

Learn more at http://www.sciencelearn.org/milky-way

The earth's great whales and other sea going creatures feast on tiny plankton, massive bears eat berries and roots, towering giraffes thrive on leaves and other vegetation. Insects. Reptiles. Fish. Mammals.

How many species and variations of plants exist? And this "creator" put so much detail into the intricate designs found in the most mundane of things.

Consider a drop of water. To the naked eye it's just a clear fluid.

Raindrop on a Frond by Louise Docker
Photograph (used by permission)
http://lookingglassimages.wix.com/lookingglassphotography

In just a teaspoon of pond water we can find a small world of its own. The government of Canada states, "Even a drop of water is an aquatic ecosystem, since it contains or can support living organisms." So instead of studying the whole lake, much can be learned in a laboratory by putting one drop of water at a time under a microscope.

Natural chemicals. Nutrients. Amino Acids. Minerals. How many combinations of these things can be found? How much is there about this lavish world that has not even been discovered yet? Every single, discreet portion and every subatomic particle a scientist has ever studied appears to have a purpose. Everything accomplishes something. If you remove any one thing from our natural world, something else—and perhaps many other things—will be affected.

Now when you cut a forest, an ancient forest in particular, you are not just removing a lot of big trees and a few birds fluttering around in the canopy. You are drastically imperilling a vast array of species within a few square miles of you. The number of these species may go to tens of thousands . . . Many of them are still unknown to science, and science has not yet discovered the key role undoubtedly played in the maintenance of that ecosystem, as in the case of fungi, microorganisms, and many of the insects.

-E. O. Wilson (quoted in Wikipedia
http://en.wikipedia.org/wiki/E._O._Wilson)

The effects on those other elements will cause another change in something else.

Every "thing" in nature has a purpose.

CHAPTER 2

Pondering Out Loud

With all of the knowledge gathered over millennia of research and study, the deeper meaning of life still remains a mystery.

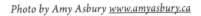

Photo by Amy Asbury www.amyasbury.ca

We know that a person can choose to believe; we can choose to believe anything. The very definition of choice makes it our decision. But when it comes to faith, there are only a few streams of thought that most of us seem to fit into. Most people, regardless of the river we swim in, can accept that all of the natural things we have found in the world were designed for a purpose. One question that divides us squarely into two camps is, "Was there a person/being involved in the design process?"

I just bought a small drill bit that was produced to remove screws that have been stripped or have broken off in a piece of wood or other substance: $8.50. It has a small and specific purpose. This bit was designed to accomplish something. Somebody took the time to imagine, experiment, and construct it. The inventor came across a problem. Wood screw: stripped and un-removable.

Then she (or he, I don't know which) came up with a plan to create something that could solve the problem. A calculated design!

We can choose to believe that natural things were designed by Someone. Or we can subscribe to the conviction that nature was created by Nature herself. But of course we know—rather, we choose to believe—that Nature herself is not actually a self.

Nevertheless . . . . If Nature has no one directing her, and if she is not a self who could choose a direction, then the choice left to us is to believe that all of the amazing complexity of Nature was designed by No One. So then we have differing opinions and beliefs. Do both sides base their arguments on belief? No. A person says in his heart, "There is no God," and then sets out to use his brain to prove it. And vice versa, of course. It is a matter of heartfelt belief. The mind follows. Can anyone prove either side? Not so far as we know. Therefore, we are left to choose what we believe.

Right in the midst of my own lifelong faith, I have been questioning everything.

From that very point, I have asked myself, "What would I do if I was God?"

Maybe, If I Was God, I would create human beings who would spend their days floating, not unlike the blobfish, except it would be in a warm, soothing fluid. No pressure. No requirements. Our muscles would be supported and held up with a gentle pressure from every angle. Happy little beings just floating and feeling good!

Or perhaps Nature would bend to my every desire. There would be no pain, because anyone could adjust his or her individual reality to fit our quest for comfort.

I could hope for "a world that was self-sustaining, in which we passively spent our days as consumers instead of contributors," (*The End of Religion* by Bruxy Cavey) www.bruxy.com

Is that what you would do? Can you imagine that kind of reality? Nothing required of us. Nothing withheld from us. All things are ours for the asking. What kind of people would we be? Would I want to have children who lack nothing and have no responsibility? In Chapter 4, we will take a serious look at how struggle and difficulty shape character.

Throughout our history, we have said that God told us to do a lot of strange things.

If I Was God . . .

I wouldn't send my people out on Crusades to eradicate the heathen.

I wouldn't ask them to fight holy wars.

I wouldn't round up First Nations children and put them in Canadian residential schools to make them Christian.

I wouldn't go to Africa and bring people of a different colour across an ocean to make them slaves of so-called Christians.

I wouldn't have televangelists pouring out alligator tears to lift some cash from good-hearted people.

I wouldn't do a lot of things that all religions have done that clearly do not reflect the heart of a good, creative Anyone.

Also, I wouldn't make an impossible-to-follow list of laws that restrict and impose burdens until faith has lost its meaning.

While my people were still barbaric and evolving, I might consider educating them in what foods to eat. I might say, "Don't eat pork. It's easy to get sick from it if you don't cook it well." I could suggest people don't drink too much alcohol or coffee. Perhaps I would teach that everything can be done in moderation. I think, as a god, I might find it my "parental responsibility" to inform my "children" of the dangers of all sorts of things.

Today, in Toronto, Canada, while standing in line at a Greyhound bus depot, I was waiting my turn to make my complaint about schedules. There on a hard seat sat a man with eyes closed, pointer fingers touching his thumbs. Deliberately seeking peace through meditation in the midst of the chaos. I immediately calmed down, knowing his was the way of peace.

If I was God, I would suggest people meditate or practice clearing their minds, emptying themselves of all attitudes and opinions to make room for love and compassion. Everybody could benefit from a bit of inner peace. And if there's no compassion, life is empty.

However, if our meditation only serves to empty our minds, and if it simply causes one to feel and do nothing at all . . . well, there could be some hesitation to propose that.

Because if you are

　　Not hurting anyone

　　Not hating anyone

Not killing anyone

Not committing adultery

Not speaking falsely to anyone, not lying

Not stealing from anyone

Nor even injuring anyone in any way . . .

If you are avoiding pitfalls only because you are not interacting with anyone, that also means you are not loving anyone either. If I Was God . . . I would encourage everyone to be engaged and relating with others.

I wouldn't be watching from my perch, waiting to correct everything a person does wrong. I would not be trying to catch you in the act.

Harry Emerson Fosdick wrote about a poster representing God to children: a big eye looking down from the clouds. He writes, "That kind of bogey god is not worthy of an honest man's worship."

I also wouldn't pour out guilt like rain and, at the same time, I could not be a mindless energy in the universe giving gifts to everyone who asked in just the right way.

How much is unfounded in contemporary religious thought? How can we release our minds from the hold on us?

Now, If I Was God, I think I would have to leave it up to people to decide for themselves what they believe. To be a true friend to those who are close to us, we have to allow them the right to be themselves. Otherwise we lose trust. What kind of God would enforce loyalty? Or conformity? Or any kind of servitude?

If I Was God . . . I would be right here. And if you didn't believe it, well, that wouldn't make me any less present. Nor would it diminish my desire to be your friend. When humanity believed the world to be flat, it remained round in spite of our beliefs. Conversely, my faith can never create a real God.

If I Was God . . . I would want to have conversations with my beings. Real relationships. I would long to be close to them and be friends. Together, we would look deeply at the world I had created for them. I would say, "Get out of the city for a while. Take a casual drive along a country road. Look at the explosion of nature. Or walk down a city street. Check out the everyday, ordinary-looking people. Look deeply into someone's eyes. Find the real person."

If I had made them, if I had invented the concept of humanity, if I was truly the Father/Mother of us all, then I would be so in love with my people. Can you see what I mean? I occasionally do something artistic. I create something beautiful and, oh man, I swell up with pride. Imagine if I had made the beauty that is you. I have kids. They're a little strange, but you gotta know that I think that they are the greatest thing ever.

If I Was God . . . I would also know that even though they are the Prima Inventora, humans are not always GOOD. Humans crash around and bump into one another.

Three little boys were playing at Johnny's house. In the rec room, they started to fight over the toys. One child pushed another, colliding with a table, they toppled his mother's favourite lamp. The colourful globe shattered before them.

She sat the trio down and talked about what had just happened. Together, they stared at the floor. Finally, she said, "Listen, guys I really liked that lamp. Now that you've broken it, I'll have to go buy another one. I can never replace it, but I'll forgive you. Let's try to play nicely with each other, okay?"

All, in turn, said they were sorry; however, one boy also argued, "But it wasn't my fault!"

Johnny's mother said, "Let's not blame each other anymore. Let's forgive and forget about it. We'll try to be better from now on, okay?"

Two of them agreed, but the other repeated, "It wasn't my fault."

"Why don't you go outside and play? You can still have some fun today."

They went out, but he kept insisting. "It wasn't my fault." Finally, he wandered home alone. Johnny and his other friend had a great time.

Once in a while a small face would appear in a window, just watching. A young, lonely face, holding on to his innocence, all by himself.

As adults, the bumps and scrapes have greater consequences. If I Was God . . . I would be constantly creating opportunities to let go and start over.

Here's a wild question.

If There Was a God . . . Would She Be a He?

You might think this to be somewhat trivial. But centuries of male dominance suggest that much damage has been done, and therefore some consideration is necessary. By no strange coincidence have we come to embrace more male gods than female deities. What is up with that? We know that, at the time many of the gods we continue to take seriously were just taking shape, we were a world community of thinking, breathing, wondering, worshipping, seeking patriarchs. Men. That's right. Males were in charge.

When humanity first realized the idea of individual power and strength, we then noticed that one gender was stronger than the other.

We realized that one gender, the male, could literally force the female counterpart to do the will of the other. That's right. Oh! And then there was that other thing: child bearing. And that other, other thing kept women down several days every month. We men decided to exploit that. Not all of us. Not all of the time. But just enough to remain boss. All of that is finally changing. Note that most of our images of God are male because gods are supposed to be strong.

An ancient Bible writer actually wrote, "God is not a man that he should lie." Not a man, but a He? We did not know how to interpret that. "He" is not a man. We are faced, then, with a very important question. But our first consideration is not . . . Is God female? Rather . . . If there is a God, wouldn't that God be another type of gender? Or a non-gendered being? Perhaps God, if there is such a thing, is a whole being of some kind. Maybe no one has ever seen God and we just don't know anything about Her/His anatomy.

Wouldn't a good God be a creator that makes both genders equal and equally able to approach said God?

Consider what I call the "created" gods: the myths. When we imagined them, we made them so human. The real God, if there is one, would already have been whatever God is long before we postulated anything. This "God" would not have needed genitalia. Would He have been male in personality only? Wouldn't She be the Mother of us all? It is entirely possible then that it was the dominant human males who decided that God must also be male.

Although we have some valid speculation, we have no proof of what kind of being our Creator might be. However, for our purpose, we should move past the male/female debate.

In the areas of faith and religion, we need to do serious, concentrated research. The title of Rob Bell's book *Velvet Elvis, Repainting the Christian Faith*, says it all. We need to re-open the conversation of what it means to have faith. We cannot just accept what our parents believed. In every area of human study, every generation finds new information. It is quite impossible to become stagnant. Unfortunately, in the religious world, there is strong motivation to hold to the ways and means that have been accepted for generations.

However, every person and each new community needs to own its own faith. No one can say the old ways were wrong. Nor are they completely irrelevant. What can be said is this: children and young adults of the

21st century do not think like any other generation ever has. There is no way for them to view life from a previous vantage point. They are not growing up in the mid-to-late 20th century like I did.

The question is: are you willing to join the conversation?

People are asking. Answers are being presented. Will your voice be heard?

There is no value in rejecting the inquiries.

Tell me all your thoughts on God. 'Cause I'd really like to meet Her.

CHAPTER 3

Questions – The Dark Chapter

Roman poet and philosopher Lucretius wrestled with questions regarding the possibility of a Divine Creator. "Had God designed the world, it would not be a world so frail and faulty as we see."

Picture this fictional event, which has played out in different ways for many brave men and women.

On the tarmac, Richard rolls his wheelchair away from the plane at a Canadian airport. He just about made it through his third tour of duty in Afghanistan. Eight days, seven hours, and forty-three minutes before he was scheduled to come home, his vehicle drove over a roughly constructed roadside bomb. The left leg has been amputated just below the knee.

This young father has seen horrors he never wants to talk about. He is a hero, who not only gave his time and risked his life, but joins the ranks of those who have paid the almost-ultimate price. His family connection and his mental health are now both at risk.

Richard's wife stands outside, waiting for the officials to greet her wounded husband. Their two-and-a-half year old son can't wait. He bolts across the wet pavement to go see his Dadda, who has been away for most of his life. He slips and crashes face first onto the pavement, peeling skin off of his left cheekbone.

The anxiety that has been lurking just below the surface is more than Beth can control. She drops to her knees beside her son, sobbing. Heaving under the load of her overburdened heart, she has no strength to raise the boy in her arms. Grandma comes to the toddler's rescue.

This was supposed to be a day to feel proud, an event to honour a hero. The media will report it with kindness, but they cannot hide the tragedy we read about all too often in the local paper. This little family is living it out one agonizing moment at a time.

We all know that life, for some, can be difficult beyond description.

If you need a solution with seven easy steps, then go to the self-help section of the local book store. Study and find paths that work for you. But in the meantime, I still have questions that go unanswered.

Question: If there is a God, why does he allow evil?

Wars destroy the lives of millions of people year after year.

See http://en.wikipedia.org/wiki/List_of_wars_by_death_toll

Here are three examples.

Death Toll - Second World War - between 60,000,000 and 78,000,000

Death Toll - Second Congo War, 1998 to 2003 - between 2,500,000 and 5,400,000

Death Toll - Afghanistan, 1979 to present - 3,000,000 and counting

The partnership of anger and greed makes life for millions of innocent people a living hell on earth . . . and is big business.

Example - great wealth is accumulated in the sale of arms supporting war. It is estimated that over 1.5 trillion dollars is spent yearly on military expenditures worldwide (2.7% of World Gross Domestic Product).

Canada and Brazil are reported to be in the Top 10 World GDP Countries List: Canada with GDP of $1.4 trillion and Brazil with $1.3 trillion.

In other forms of evil, animals suffer and whole species are becoming extinct because of human excess. Children's lives are destroyed for a few moments of sexual pleasure. The environment is exploited. Rivers, lakes, and oceans are polluted with industrial waste in order to preserve a profitable bottom line.

There has been a battle in the courts attempting to stop a mining company from dumping 400,000 tonnes of toxic tailings a year into Sandy Pond, a pristine lake in Newfoundland previously known for its prize-winning trout (www.http://sandypondalliance.org).

The Alberta Oil Sands continue to use Mother Earth as storage for tailings.

Question: Why doesn't God do something to put an end to the ravages of poverty?

According to the World Hunger Education Service, in 2010 there were 925 million hungry people. By definition, world hunger refers to "the want or scarcity of food in a country. The related technical term is malnutrition. - Malnutrition is a general term that indicates a lack of nutritional elements necessary for human health to the one the lack of protein . . . and food that provides energy . . .

Protein-energy malnutrition (PEM) is the most lethal form of malnutrition/hunger. It is basically a lack of calories and protein. . . .

Children are the most visible victims of under-nutrition. Children who are poorly nourished suffer up to 160 days of illness each year." www. http://worldhunger.org

What are the causes of hunger?

The World Education Service provides the following points for consideration:

1. Poverty is the principal cause of hunger.

2. Harmful economic systems are the principal cause of poverty and hunger.

3. Conflict is a cause of hunger and poverty.

Man-made poverty – the result is hunger and death.

An alien planet sent scouts to examine Earth. They visited all of our countries and moved among us without us knowing that they were even here. Upon noticing the vast difference between the wealthy and the poor, they asked how this could be. "Why do you allow so many people to suffer? You have so much that you can't even use."

Our answer: "Oh, we don't share like that. People have to take care of themselves."

If I Was God . . . I would cry.

Question: If there is a God who knows all and sees all, didn't He or She know beforehand that we would do this?

Even though I was well aware of the responsibility that must be shouldered by humanity, If I was God, I might be tempted to feel like a failure for all of the pain inherent in our world. After all, this would be my project, so to speak. If I Was God . . . would I not stop this before it even started?

It appears as though people could solve these problems by themselves. Therefore, if we assign to God some of the responsibility, we still know that we can fix the problems if we want to. Humans are behaving badly.

We might successfully argue that all of the above is avoidable. These tragedies are products of the choices we have made. We may be absolutely correct in saying, "You can't blame God."

If we, the caretakers of our world, would practice generosity, these things would not happen. Perhaps it's not such a bad idea to love you neighbour as much as we love ourselves.

Question: Why do so-called acts of God hurt so many people year after year?

We can't blame a tsunami on Wall Street. No, it just happens, and if you just happen to be in the wrong place, then tragedy just happens to you. Do floods, earthquakes, and tornadoes come because of our laziness? Are they acts of punishment from an angry God?

Question: What kind of a God would let these tragedies occur? Is this the way a good Creator would want life to be?

In my thirties, I had a friend whose life was great. A bright future lay ahead. He was financially comfortable and happy. He had a beautiful wife and family. Someone insisted that he would not be such a happy guy without the financial security he enjoyed. I argued that there was something deeper lifting him to his obvious contentment. Within a year of that conversation, at the age of thirty-four, he was diagnosed with cancer. Greg was beyond brave; he was expectant. A most courageous person through it all, he was actually looking forward to meeting his God, who was "waiting to greet him on the other side." He died after suffering for about a year. I loved

I submit that we will all be faced, one day, with the hardship of a lifetime. All of us. No one gets out alive. M. Scott Peck began his megasuccessful book *The Road Less Travelled* with the very short sentence, "Life is difficult."

If there is a God, then we have to wonder. We have to ask these questions and more. Are life's mysteries a conundrum to only a few of us? At this point, I refuse to reach into the file cabinet filled with quick responses to placate those who don't want to deal with not knowing. Whether the pain is caused by Nature and allowed by a Creator, or the result of actions by silly humanoids, we all agree it is nonetheless pain. And it affects all people in real ways.

Question: Are we supposed to have it all figured out by now?

So many philosophers. Great thinkers. Women and men dedicated to research in the human sciences. Yet we wander, aimlessly at times.

"Most men live lives of quiet desperation."
-Henry David Thoreau

This, then, brings us to the universal question.

Why?
Is there any purpose in all of this? We are learning, maturing, and becoming better creatures. So what? Eventually we'll become dust. We will soon be fertilizer to make better gardens.

No one could have imagined that "Self Help" would rise, in just a few short decades, to a multibillion-dollar industry. In that simple fact lies an undeniable admission. We think we need help! We are afraid because much of it stems from our emptiness. There seems to be no purpose for ME.

Question: Where does this sense of hopelessness come from?

At the outset I asked, "Is the universe friendly?" Our picture of the universe and its perceived purpose - or purposelessness - permeates our worldview. Without a doubt, that perception dictates much of our behaviour.

In western civilization we are told that God is a loving Creator. However, it is said that because He is Truth, therefore He must also judge all people out of that position of pure justice. The apparent result is that He is going to punish the errant masses for eternity. We initially began to baptize babies in case they were to die young. This little act will appease God? We need to do something to stop him from torturing babies?

Question: What kind of God needs ceremony to protect children from his wrath?

Have you been told that billions of people who have never made the journey to faith will meet the creator who must dole out punishment? Is your God angry at His people? Is your God going to lose the vast majority of the children He loves? Is this good news?

I submit that the most adhered-to message of hope in the western world has been sabotaged. I would like to argue that many of the promoters of the faith have used the threat of hell as a sales tool. This kind of abuse has created an image of God that is prevalent in our thoughts and instrumental in shaping the way we view life as a whole.

These questions may be dark and overwhelming for you. I tremble at being one who is presenting such thoughts. I am a person of faith. I believe that there is great news from the Creator for all of humanity. And therefore I venture out into this territory, which smacks of heresy for some. If there is no one who is above our level of consciousness, if there is no being who has might beyond our human ability, then we are alone. And my heart and mind cannot accept that. I cannot bring myself to believe anything less than the very first One can find in the Holy Writings. There is a hidden beauty that flipped the first-century world upside down. It was such good news at the time. Oh, I want to find the reality of that message. It was obviously something worth living and dying for. And it was not just a new religion.

I also look at my surroundings. I see beauty everywhere. I see something at work in the world all around us, and I wonder, "How could all of this be without hope?"

I have come to accept mystery in the midst of unanswered questions. If by some effort we can humble ourselves under the canopy of a vast universe that, at present, is as undiscoverable as the Creator who has initiated all of this, then maybe it is worth exploring this very revealing quandary over what we would do . . . If You or I Were God.

In the next chapter we will consider our behaviour as we take a look at the world we know.

But right now, if, in your philosophising, some newfound thoughts press on you to ask for insight . . . if you realize that you are not satisfied . . .

If you are like many people and can doubt the validity of a personal revelation at the very moment you decide to share it with someone else . . .

If, when you are forced to say it out loud - if at that point - you feel the need to make sure it at least sounds sane, because you will be judged by what you say . . .

If you think you have a real question that is worth exploring . . .

Do you have enough conviction to ask?

Here are some exercises to solidify your quest for truth. Maybe you should write your ponderings down. Get them on paper. Try to formulate some comprehensive questions that you think the "Creator" really should answer. Write them out as if you were intending to present them to someone you think should know the answer. The exercise of spelling it out could be valuable.

Or, go somewhere where no one can hear you. Say it out loud. Ask the question as if someone is listening. If you're really passionate about it,

SCREAM IT OUT! Formulating the question, saying it, and expressing it makes it yours. It is your quest.

If you want to take it further, get some friends together and see what they say. (People that you can trust with your feelings and self respect.)

Perhaps you could take your quest to someone who gets paid to know this kind of stuff. See what it feels like to deal with a response. Will your inquiries be squashed? Will you be empowered?

Or . . . perhaps you would like to just read the next chapter.

CHAPTER 4

Our World As We Know It

"Besides being complicated, reality, in my experience, is usually odd. It is not obvious, not what you expect. . . . Reality, in fact, is usually something you could not have guessed." CS Lewis

---

The phone rings. The voice on the line resonates with a mid-range, male-sounding tone. There's a slight rasp; not a monotone, but rather an interesting flow that makes it almost musical. The command of diction is refreshing. It's your brother-in-law Frank.

You hang up after a pleasant conversation, and as you turn your attention to the papers on your desk, the phone alerts you to another call. The voice on the line resonates with a mid-range, male-sounding tone. There's a slight rasp; not a monotone, but rather an interesting flow that makes it almost musical. The command of diction is refreshing. It's your mother.

At that moment your four-year-old tugs at your suit coat to tell you that he spilled his milk on the cat, who turned to escape and in the process scratched the little guy just under his left eye. He's crying, and the blood dripping from his cheek is now on your freshly dry-cleaned suit. The toddler's voice resonates with a mid-range, male-sounding tone. There's a slight rasp; not a monotone, but rather an interesting flow that makes it almost musical. The command of diction is refreshing.

You look down at him and lose your composure. Before you come to reason, you find yourself scolding the boy. Your voice also resonates with a mid-range, male-sounding tone. There's a slight rasp; not a monotone, but rather an interesting flow that makes it almost musical. The command of diction is refreshing.

Actually, it's not refreshing at all, because everybody has exactly the same "twin in-foldings of the mucous membrane stretched horizontally across the larynx." In that imaginary world, everybody's vocal cords are identical. Everyone sounds the same.

But here, in the real world, there is variation in the depth of tone. We rise to praise the tenors. We mob the rock stars and weep with the sopranos. The great orators move us to action. Our vocal cords even reverberate with inflections from personal traits: fearful, confident, cheerful, despondent, and more.

To properly consider what I would do differently If I Was God, I would like to take a look at how the world works right now before we consider what we might change.

Harry Emerson Fosdick, a writer from almost one-hundred years ago, spoke plainly: no world that would serve to foster good human character and create good human beings could function without the following four elements that exist in our present world.

1. We all know that there are physical laws in place. The unchangeable and constant.

2. The need for progress is openly visible. We have stuff to fix and improve upon.

3. Every day we are faced with choices. We are stuck with free will.

4. Whether I like it or not, humanity is not just me. We are in a large community called the human race.

These elements make up our fixed, inescapable world. "Yet" he says, "these (four) things contain all the sources of our misery."

Let's look at each one individually.

1. The world we live in works because we have **natural, physical laws** creating and governing a constant, solid environment for human life. Gravity is something we can count on. You drop something, it falls. We stick to the ground. People and things do not just float away. Set your pen on the desk, and it will be there when you need it . . . unless Bob from accounting comes by and steals it.

Imagine a different kind of world where we could alter our environment. Bob steals your pen and you just think it back to your desk. You want it. Therefore, your reality is that you still have your pen. However, Bob really wants it. He wills it onto his desk and . . . . you see the problem. Take it further. You are altogether tired of working with Bob. He walks down the hall to your desk to pick up the papers you have prepared for the Johnson account, and suddenly someone else presides in your place because you have wished yourself away.

I remember distinctly, in a grade eight baseball game, a line drive that struck the principal in the face. He was standing just east of first base. There was really no time to move, and as he fell to the ground, I heard him say something. Now, most people would have cried out in pain. Some would have cursed. Others might have been angry at the batter. But this academic said, "What a thing to anticipate." Wow. That's it? What a thing to anticipate? He had no time to get out of the way. But he knew what was going to happen in that split second. He very correctly anticipated some kind of collision between his face and that softball.

Picture a man strolling down a gentle slope. Easy walking. Very little energy is required. Life is good. How would he encounter anyone else if we could all choose a similar gentle downward slope? Somebody has to be going "uphill" to meet him. Our world is a fixed reality, designed to be a solid, dependable place that we cannot manipulate. We are stuck inside its rules and regulatory systems. The laws of nature tell us that when that softball comes streaking toward your face, it will make contact. There will be blood.

2. What would life be like without **challenges demanding progress**? How soon would humanity dry up and become meaningless?

Harry Emerson Fosdick, in *The Meaning of Faith*, says, "A stagnant world cannot grow character. There must be real work to do, aims to achieve; there must be imperfections to overpass and wrongs to right. Only in a system where the present situation is a point of departure and a better situation is a possibility . . . can character grow."

A point of departure?

The need to move into a better situation?

Work to do?

Imperfections to improve upon?

Imagine a world where there was no need to achieve anything. Imagine if there was no need for progress.

In a stagnant world, Bob doesn't need to stop stealing pens. Without the need to lift someone out of any kind of difficulty, no one would have to consider helping a struggling acquaintance. Nor would we feel compelled to step out of our comfort zone to befriend her when everyone else pushes her away.

In this world, I wake up more mornings than not with a nagging sense that I haven't become the person I want to be. "I see what could be. But I also look in the mirror of what is." I need to grow up!

Imagine a world where there is absolutely no aspiration!

What is it that sends out the call to reach for a higher plain? Why must there be progress?

One simple reason: in the real world there is lack. There is need and shortfall and incompleteness.

3. We have already asked the question, "Why is there so much evil in the world?" And, as we have seen, Bob is quite annoying at work. People avoid him. He is, as they say, a jerk. What if Bob couldn't help but be more pleasant? What if we were to alter our physical laws, and we only allowed people to choose good? Imagine a world where we had restrictions on our **free will**.

A memo is sent out to every living human being: a list of free-will choices have been posted at libraries and town office buildings.

EVERY CITIZEN MUST TAKE THIS PILL AND YOU WILL BECOME MORE PLEASANT.

YOU WILL NO LONGER BE ABLE TO MAKE BAD CHOICES.

Essentially, from within our own will, we could only choose from a selection of pre-approved options in the difficult areas that we face daily.

"If character is to be real man must not, in his choice between right and wrong, be as Spinoza pictured him, '. . . a stone hurled through the air, which thinks that it is flying . . .;' he must have

some control of conduct, some genuine, . . . power of choice."
-Fosdick

If you are Bob's manager, then you will understand how things can be as you want them to be in one way and against your will at the same time. Your goal is a team of people who enjoy working together for the greater good of the company. You obviously want Bob to cooperate with other employees. But a good manager prefers people who are self-motivated. With that in mind, you give Bob and everyone else freedom. It is clearly not "your will" that Bob dump his responsibilities onto the others. You could stand over him and force the guy to keep working, but you want him to find purpose within the environment you have created. You have made it possible for Bob to make the wrong choice.

Your will allows people to go against your will.

If there is no possibility of evil, then it follows that there is no free will. If there is no free will, there is no humanity as we know it. If we remove the opportunity to choose, do we relegate ourselves to some form of automaton mindlessness?

4. We are all part of a large **community**.

How perfect the world would be if there just weren't any people in it?

How much pain is inflicted because somebody
    didn't clean up after himself,
    didn't stop at the stop sign,
    bought a gun and went on a rampage in a movie theatre, or became a leader of a country and then raped and robbed his own people?

Our present world is designed for interaction. The only way to stop confrontation, and thus the absolute necessity for compromise and negotiation, would be to eliminate community.

Have you noticed that we honour people of character? You know, the guy who is always ready to listen; who always seems to stand up for the underdog. The girl who can be counted on to do what she said she would do. We like that. We demand it from anyone who wants to be a friend. Our own attitude toward people who are flakes tells us that we approve of a world that provides situation after situation that, like us, demands good character.

Also, we love to be loved. We need to be noticed. We long to be appreciated. Oh, just watch that moment when a light comes on in a teen's life and they realize, "Somebody gets me!" We are social beings. We crave the touch of another lonely traveller. Are our imperfections our greatest assets?

Fosdick: "Love, which is the crown of character, lacking community, would be impossible."

No family of man/woman? No us. No need for love? No love.

We seem to approve of a world like the one we are living in, but yet we have legitimate complaints. I, along with you, wish dearly that it could be different. We still wonder, "Why do we have to suffer?"

So . . . Love is the crown of character. The highest attribute of humanity. Can you imagine a world without love? I submit that we could not have a good world without the difficulties arising from the imperfections of community. And if we eliminate situations of need, we eliminate the necessity for love.

In our present world physical laws are unchangeable and constant. The need for progress is openly visible. We are stuck with free will. And whether I like it or not, humanity is not just me. We are in a large community called the human race. And we approve.

I'm genuinely surprised by our findings thus far. We seem to agree with the way this world runs.

———

CHAPTER 5

What Would I Be Like... If I Was God?

John Lennon asked us to imagine a world where there was no religion. I will not pretend that all religion is good. Neither is it all bad. So can we please peel away some of the trappings that inevitably come with religious adherence?

If I Was God . . . I would make sure that everyone knew that I agreed with Mahatma Gandhi when he said that God has no religion.

And, more specifically, Bishop Desmond Tutu said, "God is not a Christian."

Like the biblical author Paul, I would know that pure, undefiled religion is to give attention to the broken-hearted, the lonely, the bereaved and all those suffering. (My paraphrase.)

I would also teach that if there is going to be any value to religious activity, it must not only include a vertical relationship (man to God), but a horizontal relationship too (amongst humanity and all of creation). Without the horizontal flow of love and compassion, community, charity, kindness, patience, and the appreciation of other created beings, religion is empty.

Religion, in the hands of evil men, is responsible for countless wars, continuing hatred, segregation, alienation, sexual abuse, prescribed poverty, caste systems, etc. The list goes on and on.

At the same time, however, people of faith (and some very good religious people) were responsible for the founding of most hospitals, educational systems, and charitable organizations of all kinds around the world. Malcolm Muggeridge, who, among other things, was an outspoken and controversial journalist, was forced to question his atheism/agnosticism when he visited a home that Mother Teresa founded for lepers in India. After witnessing the selfless commitment of the Sisters of Charity and random volunteers, he said something like this: "You don't ever find 'The Atheists' Homes for Orphans.' Or 'The Agnostics' Charity for the Disabled.' It's the Christians who do these things."

Does that justify the religious paraphernalia? Not even a little bit.

Compassion, charity, and kindness are all active ingredients in the making of religious activity, along with hatred, violence, and exclusion. Religious adherents can be dedicated to the point of ignoring their own needs to care for those less fortunate. And in the next breath, the lust for conformity drives them to murder those who disagree.

Little wonder then, as soon as anyone mentions God, our reference points are filled with negative images that have made the headlines in our news media. So, what are you expecting from me in this chapter? Do you expect me to be the high expression of a dying cult? Am I immaculately trained in keeping up appearances? Would an author of so-called faith like this have to maintain a squeaky clean facade? The last person you might visualise would be an average, not-so-well-dressed kind of guy who loves a good party. Like you, I am just negotiating my way through life, I haven't got it all together.

So when I ask, "What would I be like . . . If I Was God?" maybe you can picture yourself pondering the same question. We might not be that far off in our individual perceptions of what God might truly be like.

So much of western theology has concentrated on the failure of humanity; i.e. the fall of man, and therefore the necessary denial of self that leaves us wondering, "Who am I?" Maybe we haven't even arrived at that question because we are so busy asking, "Who am I allowed to be?"

As we peel away and unlearn some of what we have been inundated with, perhaps we will find deep within the human psyche a better picture of the-great-someone-out-there.

If I Was God . . . I would recognize the difference between what humans see as their potential and what we all observe in our everyday reality. I would agree with Gerry Bast, who said, "I see what could be. But I also look in the mirror of what is." We are trying so hard to be . . . something. Often it is an image we have believed we should be because it was presented to us and we bought into it. Who are you? Do you know? We wonder, "How can I be myself when I don't know myself?"

The late, great comedian Mitch Hedberg said "I think that a duck's opinion of me is highly dependent upon whether or not I have bread." That really has nothing to do with the question at hand. It's just funny! If I Was God . . . I would invent FUNNY!

Stephen Wright pondered, "You can't have everything. Where would you put it?"

If I Was God . . . I would laugh a lot. Especially at humanity. What strange, lovable creatures!

If I Was God . . . I would stand back and look at everything I had just made and say, "It is good!"

Animals, oceans, trees, fish, birds . . . I would say, "It is good!"

Humans? "Very good! VERY, VERY, VERY GOOD! You are so beautiful."

Even guys with our fat little bellies. Your partner wants to pinch that fat. Come on, smile. You know it's true.

If I Was God
I would be so confused when people would come up with
THREE SUBTLE BASICS
FOUR SPIRITUAL LAWS
FOUR PATHS TO GOD
FIVE COSMIC ELEMENTS
SIX PATHS TO GOD
NINE STEPS TO NIRVANA
PATH OF RETURN
KARMA
"D'UH! I'm right here!"

I would say "D'uh" in the nicest sort of way.

All of the above have been useful tools for living life and for finding some kind of peace. Life is hard. From time to time we all need these steps to achieve some level of wellness. But at some point humanity will be ready to shed the need for systems and find God to be as close as the sunshine on our faces and as available as the air around us.

If I Was God . . . I would be your Creator and Lover. There would be no program for being with me. Do you have a ritual you must perform to go on a first date? (Oops. Wrong question. I'll caution you do. You're trying to impress. The last thing you want is to have that person encounter the real you.) Better question - Do you have a program of activities designed to assist you with hanging out with your best friend? No.

Let me suggest we stop dressing up to approach God. Stop putting on your best face and pretending to be someone you aren't. If there is a God I'm sure we don't fool He.

Okay. Let's step back from the confrontational nature of peeling away these hindrances. I have been questioning everything. Let's do something positive.

Wherever you are right now . . . if I am God, I am with you. Breathe. If I am God, I am in that breath of air. Breathe. Draw in and say, "Yah," feel the rush of wind above your tongue, breathe out and whisper "Weh."

Breathe in, "Yah;" out, "Weh."

Yah . . . weh. Yahweh. You are quietly calling out one of the many Hebrew names of God. Every breath we take gives us life: physical and spiritual. If I was God, I would be that close. And that, at the very least, would put me in the midst of your everyday life. When you lay your head down on your pillow, even without knowing it, you speak that name. Let that name be your mantra. Know that God is with you.

Though you make your bed in hell, I am there.

Stop. Remember me. I am thinking of you. Even if a mother could forget her children, I could never forget you.

Cast your care upon me, because I care for you.

Climb to the top of a hill and clench your fists. Roar like a lion. Shout like a barbarian warlord. If I am God, then I am the commander of the angel armies. Let's go to battle together against the forces of evil that destroy lives all around you.

Go to your neighbour who is struggling financially. Offer help. I am the one who wants to nourish and provide. You and I will work side by side. When helping someone else, you will not have to look far to find me.

Is there someone at your place of employment who is not happy? Eat lunch with him. Ask questions. Be a friend. I will be closer than you can imagine.

Do you have a friend who is working with a charity? Volunteer. Help her achieve her goals.

Are you in contact with a teen who is depressed? Everybody knows twelve or one-hundred teens who are languishing under life's anxieties. Stop and listen when they speak. Open your heart and your ears. I am there!

And if you are the one in need:
> if you could use some practical steps to lead you out of a difficulty,
> if you need help to heal,
> if you want to be set free from an addiction,
> if you need basic assistance with the onslaught of life,
> then use every means and find a path to peace.
> And breathe. Breathe. Fear Not. I will never leave you.

Don't forget to find a friend.

Are you looking for an answer to life's riddles? Do you truly believe that the universe is friendly, that somewhere out there, there is someone? Treat that Someone-Out-There the way that you would treat anyone with whom you would like to have a relationship.

Listen for a moment to what women are saying to men, "Don't you dare take me out on a date, wanting to woo me, and then follow the same steps that worked on your last girlfriend. I am not her! I am not a machine that can be manipulated. Even if you find a way to negotiate your way into my life, you will still not be reaching me. I am a person. I have my own personality. If you don't have time to get to know me, then I will move on until I find someone who does."

If I Am God, pursue me. Search for me. Like that hopeful, romantic relationship, I am not hiding. I want to be wanted. If I Was God . . . if I was the person behind it all, then you would have to know that I had a reason for creating you!

If you
look for me,
I will find you!

CHAPTER 6

—

A Reason to Create

Could the world, as we know it, be the best of all possible worlds? Maybe this is as good as it gets.

See photo and read more at http://en.wikipedia.org/wiki/Solar_flare

If I Was God . . .
With all the POWER that would make me God.

Not just "a god,
But God.

If I Was God, with all that power, I would . . .

67

I could . . . do ANYTHING!

I would have so many ideas of what to do.

And I would not only have ideas . . .
But I would be the original IDEA!

www.fotolia.com

I would be . . .

The first THOUGHT.
I would be . . . The very first flow of mind energy . . . ever!

And with my power . . .

Wait – hold it.

Not only power . . .

But DESIRE . . .
And . . .

Not only desire . . . but WILL!

Bear with me . . . . Not only the will to accomplish . . .

But also the intellect, the knowledge

Actually . . . the ULTIMATE GENIUS . . .

To perform perfectly,

To create.

Just Imagine . . . I AM . . . . There is nothing else.

I AM.

I AM . . . but where am I? Am I in a . . .

Am I . . . in . . . anything?

If there is nothing . . . not even a little speck.
I mean . . . absolute void. Even blackness is something. Think . . .
nothing. Not even one tiny spot.

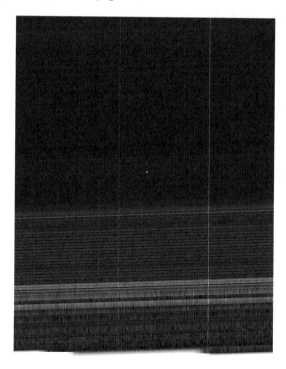

If I AM and there is nothing, but me . . . WHERE.

Could there be an END to that nothing?

How could nothing have an end?

Is there a START to nothingness?

Could there be a BEGINNING?

THERE IS NOTHING! EXCEPT ME!

I AM . . . the beginning

I AM . . . the end

If I Was God

I would BE . . .

THE POWER that could create.

I would BE . . . the original, ultimate IDEA

With the WILL and all of the GENIUS

To CREATE!

If I Was God

When I created things

Would those things that I create be in anything?

If I created, say, a universe (just for the sake of argument)

Would there be an end to that universe?

Some kind of border . . .

Where everything stops?

Or

Would there be no discovering of an end

To my creation?

An end to my universe?

Or a beginning?

What would the universe be in? And if it was in something . . .

How big would the thing be that my universe is in?

Would my UNIVERSE CONTAINER have a border where it stops?

If so, what would the container be in?

What would be on the outside of the container?

If I Was God . . .

My creation would be endless.

And I would create.

Well, at least I think I would.

You know – I would be the original idea.

I would be exploding with thoughts.
With all of the smarts to do . . . WHATEVER! ANYTHING!
And I would also be the original desire

Therefore I would want to make something . . .

But

What would I build?

Why would I build anything?

Would I have a purpose for building?

If I AM . . .

Then I am the purpose.

Should I build something?

Perhaps a birdhouse . . .

Would there be any reason

To build a bird house

If there were no birds?

Would there be any reason

To create

A bird?

Would I create a bird just so I would have reason to build a really nice birdhouse?

Wouldn't the bird be the reason for the house?

And not the house the reason for the bird?

You might say, "I've got this house, therefore I need a tenant."
If I am at all good and smart enough to build the first bird, the need for a tenant could not be my purpose;

I have this beautiful house, I had better get something to live in it!

Okay, having said that, what kind of God would I be if I created a bird and didn't provide for it?

What if there were no bird things for this bird?

Let me think . . . bird things . . .

Like trees! Birds without trees?

Trees without rain?

Trees without sunlight . . . or sunlight without energy?

And no insects for the bird to eat?

Or . . . birds without stomachs to digest.

Would there be any purpose for digestion without the desire to provide nutrition?

Nutrition that would nourish my bird.

Nourishment . . .

Causing my bird to flourish.

I am then the original desire to nourish.

If I was God . . .

I would create! Yes, I've decided! I would create. And I would build into every thing the stuff that makes my creation flourish.

My creation . . . my family.

I desire. I want my family to grow.

I want all things to grow . . .

And grow . . . and grow . . . and grow some more!

Flourish! I want all things to do well.

To be well.

I would supply the ingredients.

To make . . . every thing saturate with energy.

Yes! Energy . . .

If I am God

Then I Am

The original energy.

I am . . . the life.

My life . . . my energy . . .

Would be the original ingredient.

The original building block.

My energy would be the stuff that every "thing" is made of.

I would create life.

Life . . . living . . . breathing . . . thinking . . .

Wow! What a concept! Living beings. Life.

If I was God . . .

All things I would create would need a house . . .

Not just the bird.

A home for my all of my created things.

A huge house.

A whole world for my created beings.

Everything would grow everywhere.

Could it be a flat world?

http://www.absolute3d.net/fr/fond-ecran/paysage/Nuit/Night.jpg.html

What would be under the flat house?

Would there be a barrier on the edge of this house?

Should there be a fence around my world?

What about a cube-shaped world?

What would keep my family from falling off?

If I was God . . .

I think I would have to make a round world.

http://en.wikipedia.org/wiki/File:BlueMarble-2001-2002.jpg

And something would make everyone equal.

No part of it would be the top.

No part would be the bottom.

And something would hold my beings on the floor of their house.

My living, moving, walking family

In their massive home.

Built into this home,

Something would pull them down.

And it would hold my world together.

Pulling my family down and holding them on the floor.

But it should not be pulling so hard that they cannot move.

Nor too soft a pull.

So that my family would float away.

And someday my family would call it . . .

Gravity!

Gravity would keep my family in their home.

Perfect gravity.

Making the precise amount of pull to hold my world together.

Precision design.

Absolutely perfect!

When I watched gravity work for the first time . . . when I saw that my design had worked . . . when it could be proven that the pull of gravity was proportional to the size and density of each object . . .

I would say, "Gravity is good!"

If I was God...

My family would be held safely on the Earth.

If I was God...

When I built my world...

Right at the beginning I would build something deep into the fabric of Creation. I would plant it into the very essence of my universe.

It would be like planting a seed that later grows up into a tree that eventually becomes a place for my family to find shade. That seed would gradually grow into a place for them to feel safe. Not just a physical shrine that they would have to journey to, but rather a place of refuge deep in the depths of their being.

I would build into my world, right into the very hearts of my family, the seed that would eventually produce all that I desire for them. It would be like putting yeast into a huge amount of flour. It would slowly expand until it filled every heart, just like yeast works its way into every part of the dough.

I would build into my creation a seed, a hope within my family that would slowly work its way through the whole lump of my creation until my desire for their well-being filled everything.

I would create the Earth.

Round, beautiful, growing,

Nourishing.

All areas equal... equal... but not the same.

No two areas would be the same.

Would it be safe? Hmmmm . . . safe?

Of course some areas would not be safe.

Heights and depths.

Rushing, crashing, rising, and falling.

It would be wild and dangerous.

Not safe . . . but good!

How would I start all of this?

I would, in my desire for Life, formulate my idea.

Like an engineer seeing the final picture of what he is designing,
Like the knowledge that the "whole oak tree" is in the acorn,
Like a tiny seed that can grow up into a tree where birds can nest,
The whole of Creation would be IN my original idea.

Has anyone ever tried to measure a thought? Does an active and working idea in someone's mind have matter? We know it has energy. If it contains matter, it might just be smaller than any of the subatomic particles we have found.

I Am . . . and I am ready to create. The idea is now fully formed in my mind.
Picture this blueprint for creation. It is in the mind of a God who has all of the power needed to CREATE! A creator is poised to set in motion and ready to release, like a rocket into space, the seeds of the universe. A tsunami of energy primed to initiate all that is and all that can be. ALL of that is compressed into a thought!

If brain activity can have matter, then this thought is a like a neutron star, which weighs hundreds of millions of tons per teaspoon.

The idea is ready. It is packed! A seed is chock full of design and energy.

If I Was God . . . I would command my thought into action and there would be a bang! A big bang!

Why? Because my thought contains the idea. My will contains the power to perform it. And my word sets it in motion. When I say "Go!" it all explodes into action.

Just saying that there was a big bang is a pretty lame representation.

Imagine all of the energy that I have prepared to perform all of the work that is required to build creation. It is just a thought. However, the energy in it would be the original building block from which all things come. Setting this plan into action would require unfathomable initiative. All of the energy that could perform the work would have to be cradled in that thought! And the command would explode out into action, creating all things as it expands. Can you say "bang"?

And so with the means and the desire to create, I would make you.

footnote

http://en.wikipedia.org/wiki/Energy_(psychological)

"Mental energy has been repeatedly compared to or connected with the physical quantity energy. Studies . . . have found that mental effort can be measured in terms of increased metabolism in the brain. The modern neuroscientific view is that brain metabolism, measured by functional magnetic resonance imaging or positron emission tomography is a physical correlate of mental activity."

References[edit]

1.Jump up ^ Hall, Calvin J.; Nordby, Vernon J. (1999). A Primer of Jungian Psychology. New York: Meridian. ISBN 0-451-01186-8.

2.Jump up ^ Hall, Calvin, S. (1954). A Primer in Freudian Psychology. Meridian Book. ISBN 0-452-01183-3.

3.Jump up ^ Bowlby, John (1999). Attachment and Loss: Vol I, 2nd Ed. Basic Books. pp. 13–23. ISBN 0-465-00543-8.

4.Jump up ^ Benton, D., Parker, P. Y., & Donohoe, R. T. (1996). The supply of glucose to the brain and cognitive functioning. Journal of Biosocial Science, 28, 463–479. Fairclough, S. H., & Houston, K. (2004). A metabolic measure of mental effort. Biological Psychology, 66, 177-190. Gailliot, M.T., Baumeister, R.F., et al. (in press). Self-control relies on glucose as a limited energy source: Willpower is more than a metaphor. Journal of Personality and Social Psychology.

CHAPTER 7

———

Larry and Me/God

Mahatma Gandhi lived his life on the premise that weak people do not have the strength to forgive. He chose to be different. What kind of God would not have that depth of character?

A person I once knew took his own life many years ago. Let's call him Larry.

If I Was God . . . When Larry showed up at my door after he had passed on from the physical world, he would find himself having to climb up onto my doorstep to face me. Fresh from his episode, he would come face to face with the One who gave him life. Up those stairs he would climb to that front door, where everybody has to knock and wait for the One who knows to answer.

If I Was God . . . it would be appointed for all people to die. And then I, the God who made them, the Creator who loved the very thought of each person, would have to judge them. Every single human being.

Nobody would escape the light that reveals his or her innermost thoughts.

If I Was God . . . it wouldn't be my desire for any life to be wasted or taken from me. Not even one insignificant, unknown, lonely person. Insignificant to some people, perhaps, but not to me.

If I Was God . . . you would know that I made everyone, and no one is insignificant.

When Larry showed up at my door, I would know that he wasn't going to be like some people. No. When some people see who opened the door, they would be so angry. You see, many would recognize me as the voice that had been nudging them forward all of their lives. Not criticizing. Just showing them the better person they could be. Some would hate me for calling them to change, to rise, to be something more. Some would have preferred to be left alone in their selfish pursuits.

Others will recognize me and say, "That was you? All this time you have been showing me how to live life well! Oh I am so glad to meet you. You're a real being? Ha-ha-ha-ha-hallelujah!"

Larry would recognize me right away as the voice that, at one time in his life, had been a lot clearer to him. When he was a much younger child, when Larry was a little boy, he could hear me in the darkest night. He could hear my whisper when the terrors that haunted his house were more than he could handle. All the sadness, all that depression and self hatred is more than a child should ever have to hear about, never mind having to bear on his tiny shoulders.

Oh man! If I Was God . . . you wouldn't want to make me angry. But some of the things that people do to children—I hate to think about it. I wouldn't want to be God and be as angry as I could get thinking about it.

But when Larry became a teenager and my reassuring voice had been silenced by his total disdain for himself and the self-loathing that he had been taught, he began to hate everything that he thought he was.

When he showed up on my front steps and I opened the door, he would recognize me as the one who had said, "I am right here. Don't be afraid."

Yeah. He would recognize me all right.

Following is the shortened version of what my encounter with Larry might be like. The process might actually take decades to unfold.

Of course, at my house, we won't be bound up in TIME.

Nope.

If I Was God . . .

I would get rid of that immediately.

Larry would see me. "Ohhhh! It's you! Oh please don't hate me." He would hold his arm up to shield himself from my light. "I should have listened to you. I'm such an idiot. I hate myself! You were right there. I should have—"

"Larry. Larry! Hey. Stop."

"I screwed up so bad."

"Everybody does. You don't hate yourself. You don't even know yourself."

"What is going to happen to me?"

"What do you want to happen?"

"Does that matter? I'm such a—"

I would stop him. "Don't think thoughts like that about yourself, Larry."

"I was afraid of everybody. Nobody wanted to be my friend. Even that family that went to the church near us didn't know what to do with me. I was just a freak!"

"You're right. They had no idea what to do. They were just a little overwhelmed. I told them to love you. But there are very few who really get it."

"What's going to happen to me?"

"What do you want to happen?"

"Cut the psychology crap!" Larry would scream, realizing it was all over. Tension and anxiety boiling inside. His life done. He had made his choice.

"Where do I have to go? Am I going to hell? Every suicide goes to hell, don't they?"

"I'll be the judge of that."

Silence.

"That was a joke, Larry. It's impolite not to laugh when God tells a joke."

"Come on! Let's get this over with."

"Well. Maybe I should call Judge Judy. She's fast! I'm sorry, Larry, couldn't resist."

At that point he would look deep into my eyes. Searching. "You really aren't angry at me, are you?"

"Nope."

"Oh for crying out loud! What am I going to do?"

"Well now, I like that question better. Have a peek inside my front door."

Larry would lean forward and, If I Was God, he would see inside MY HOUSE, where there would be a whole lot of people mingling. If I was God . . . my house would be filled with all kinds of people: all nationalities, with all sorts of religious affiliations. People with no religious connections and no religion at all would be together in my house. Then he would see that other guy who killed himself in his little town.

"What is he doing here? How did he get in?"

"What do you mean?"

"Why would you invite him to your house? I heard he had a lot going for him." Then, pausing to find his point, Larry would ask, "What did he have to feel sorry for himself about?"

"Is that why you took your life? You felt sorry for yourself?"

"Uhhh. No. Not like that. My life was hell."

"Now that is the truth. Somebody made your life a real hell. But you, my friend, you were drowning in your own self-pity."

"Do you know how they treated me? I didn't have a prayer."

"That's an opening for another joke, but okay Larry, let's be serious. What did they do to you?"

I would allow the anger to rise again inside the young man as he relived the pain. "They made life so hopeless! So useless! I didn't have a chance!"

Very softly, I would say, "Yes you did. And yes I do know what they did to you. I was there."

"What? You were there? Why didn't you stop them?"

"The same reason I didn't stop you from turning it on yourself. I only gave you the option. And I offered you the courage. They chose to hate you because they despised their own weakness. Your parents hated themselves and they turned it on you. Then, following suit, you chose to hate yourself . . . and them."

"I didn't hate them."

"Yes you did."

"No, I didn't!"

"Yes you did."

"Stop saying 'Yes you did.' I didn't hate them."

"Yes you did."

"I did?"

"Yes. I'm sorry, but you did. Remember that last thought you had? What were you thinking just before you turned the gun on yourself and pulled the trigger?"

And right there, on my porch, at that very juncture, a knowing look would come over Larry's face. "I wanted them to know how bad they hurt me. I hoped this would finally get through to them. You're right. Son of a—"

Gently again. "Yes you did."

"Yes I did. I really did. You knew it too. I'm so sorry. I really messed up their lives, didn't I?"

"Well, that's another story. If you decide to stay with us, maybe I'll let you come to the door with me when they arrive."

"What? What did you say?"

"You heard me, Larry. You can come greet them with me."

The shock on Larry's face is a photo I keep on my wall of great moments. "I mean . . ." he fumbled for a clear thought. "No. Not that! If I decide to stay with you. Is that what you said?"

"Yes I did."

"If I decide? I can't stay with you here! I'm so . . . I'm so . . ."

"What?"

"I'm so sorry. I should have . . . done something. I should have left home. I should have gone to that church family. They let lots of people into their house. Weird people. I should have gone to the police, the hospital, anywhere else! I could have. But I didn't. Instead I stayed in my crazy house. I just couldn't believe that—"

"Yes you could have, Larry. You had faith."

Right there Larry would stop and stare into my eyes again. Digging deeper into his soul than ever before. "You're right. There were times when I knew I could just walk out and never come back. Why didn't I?"

"You were lazy."

"Lazy?"

"Yep. It was easier just to wallow in your sorrow."

"Lazy! Lazy? You don't let up, do you?"

"It's really quite impossible for me to tell a lie." I would say, "I was there the whole time. You chose to feel sorry for yourself."

"But—"

"No buts, Larry. Nobody feels the need to smoke here."

"What?"

"Just 'cause I'm God doesn't mean everybody gets my jokes. No saying 'but' here, okay? Here we face up to the truth. No trying to get around it." Long pause. "Okay?"

"Okay. Geez!"

"That's me."

"What?"

"Never mind, Larry. Never mind."

"Really. I do remember. I wallowed in that feeling that I got when I would sit and cry over my own problems. Man. I didn't realize I was . . . wait." A twinkle in his eye for the first time since he walked up to my door. "Don't say it. I guess I did know it. I knew that I was just soaking in self-pity. Bathing in it. Nobody loves Larry! Wah wah!"

"Larry? Now you're the joker."

"I know! I never kidded around back . . . umm . . . back there. I am feeling better! What did you do to me?"

"Some people tell me it's the fresh air we have here."

Larry would look around at the scenery outside my house, in my yard. "I honestly do not remember the last time I felt this good! I'm feeling kinda clean inside."

"You know what? Someday I'll show you when it was that you felt just this good. But right now you've got a decision to make."

"I do?"

"Yes you do, Lawrence. There's a real shindig going on in my house!"

"A shindig? What?"

"I throw the best parties, Larry-Man! And you're invited!"

"I'm invited?"

"You know it, mister! And you wanna know what else?"

"What? What?" Larry would be looking like he was going to pee himself.

"Everybody here is just dying to see you. I've been telling them that you're coming. Well, they're not dying to see you. Nobody dies here. Because I have already paid your admission."

Larry would then begin to laugh, "You paid my admission?" But he wouldn't laugh long, because he would start right away into crying and then he couldn't cry long because he'd start laughing again.

After a while everybody would find my humour irresistible, If I Was God.

"I knew it! I knew it!" he would shout. "I thought it was too good to be true! I thought it was just a myth. But then . . . I knew it had to be true." For just a split second some confusion would show on Larry's face. Then wonder and sheer joy. "You died so that I could live."

"I did, Larry. It wouldn't be the same without you here." At this point I would get the biggest hug ever.

And just as he was going to cross that line in his mind, that dividing point of contention, "But I don't deserve any of this. I'm a cry baby who never did anything for anybody. I just felt sorry for myself all of my life and then took away the very breath you gave me."

"Yes you did."

"I didn't go to church. I didn't pray for anybody. I didn't become a Christian. I—"

"There are a lot of people doing a lot of things, and they think it's going to buy them a ticket to my party. But they never let me get to know who they really are. I don't even know them. Larry, it's not my will that any of my kids should miss out on life. And everybody is going to stand on this porch, and they will have to look into a mirror that reveals all of the ego that they have sheltered in their hearts. Just like you did."

Another hug. More bewilderment. Some tears. A crazy, clumsy dance. And then a flop down on his butt onto an old wooden chair on my porch.

And this time, when Larry looked up at me with the most amazing transformation on his face, I would say, "You look younger, Larry. And yet more mature. So confident, and at the same time . . . kind of childish. Kind of like you're starting over!" I would not be able to remember anyone who was so good-looking.

Then, with a mischievous raising of one eyebrow, Larry would say to me, "So . . . what are we waiting for? Are you coming in?"

"Ha!" Right there, it would be my turn to shed a few tears. "Yes I am, Larry. Let's go."

If I Was God, Larry and I would forget all about those other years. He would be more than just safe here. Nobody would change Larry's mind about who he is and what he is worth after he enters into my house!

Oh, and you know what else? We would party like it was Saturday night every night!

Larry would have so many friends If I Was God.

CHAPTER 8

Light, Darkness, Round Worlds, and Mud... Then Beauty and More

Martin Luther King Jr. followed in Ghandi's footsteps and faced down hatred with love. He didn't presume to curse the darkness. Rather he shone a light in his world to contrast racial violence and segregation.

LIGHT

If I Was God . . . I would create light. I would design a means of making things visible, of illuminating all things. The idea of light emanating from bright globes is a pretty good one, don't you think? Perhaps I should create huge, smelting furnaces that are continuously on fire. Goodness gracious, great balls of fire blasting light into the sky to shine on everything, everywhere. Is that a great idea or what? Oh, wait a minute. That is our world as we know it.

If I am to consider doing things differently, my proposals will have to be better than what exists presently. But how could I beat the home we have. Right now there are immeasurable generators of light, heat, and energy in a sky that seems to be perfectly orchestrated and completely balanced. And it's as though someone knew that all of these solar systems pumping heat would raise the temperature to a disastrous level if they were just stagnant. So, apparently by some fluke of Nature or an act of Intelligence our galaxies are moving swiftly away from one another in the ever-expanding universe, thus dispersing the heat at the perfect rate to keep us from burning up. I really don't think anyone will be able to upgrade that bit of genius.

There is a planet who's attending sun burns at more than 15 million Kelvin. It is thought to be hotter than 85% of all of the stars in the Milky Way. The visible and invisible radiation is so intense that, during an eclipse, if a person were to look at it for just a few seconds, it would cause damage to his or her eyes, even to the point of going blind. And that sun "releases energy at the mass-energy conversion rate of 4.26 million metric tons per second" and "9.192 megatons of TNT per second."

However, the distance from that orb to its blazing star gives scientists hope that it could support life. Also, the ultraviolet rays appear to be filtered. Maybe we could travel there. Maybe, just maybe, we could live there.

You already know about this planet. You have come to call it home. It is the beautiful blue marble called Earth.

We live on a planet where our galaxy's "sunlight is filtered through the Earth's atmosphere." More than "97% of midrange ultraviolet radiation is blocked by the ozone layer, and would cause much damage to living organisms if it penetrated the atmosphere."

The ozone layer is "approximately 20 - 30 kilometres (12 - 19 miles) above Earth" and "averages about 3 millimetres (1/8 inch) thick, approximately the same as two pennies stacked one on top of the other." http://en.wikipedia.org/wiki/Ozone_layer

(While I was editing and rewriting this book, the Canadian government stopped the circulation of pennies.)

ENERGY

That massive amount of energy is being released from our sun. Some birds and insects can see the ultraviolet rays that we cannot. We can't see the waves, but we certainly feel the effects.

Our sun is a great ball of burning gas. There is a cover over our heads (1/8" thick) keeping us from roasting. Instead of killing us, our sun is a source of life-giving energy.

Our solar star is only one of a million, trillion phenomena we call Nature. Just another of the so-called natural things in our world; the normal, everyday activity of life where you and I come from.

Consider the Andromeda Galaxy, which is not far from ours (not far in relation to a universe that may have no end.) There is a sun so large that, if it were situated where ours is, we and our whole planet would be inside it. How much heat? How much light? Who can fathom the amount of energy pouring freely into space from that little furnace? I estimate lots. Multiply these unimaginable numbers by hundreds of billions of stars in every galaxy.

The Oxford English Dictionary, in reference to physics, describes energy as "the property of matter and radiation which is manifest as a capacity to perform work." To perform work? What work is all that power accomplishing? Where does all of the energy come from? Where does it go?

So . . . yes, I would create light. And I can't imagine a more perfect design than the one we know. If I were to build a home for the likes of you and I, I would want energy to blast out from heavenly bodies in the sky just like the ones adorning the heavens above us. And the light that shines on the home that I provide will be filled with my energy. I will be the source. And the result will be life itself.

Now, we do know that nothing can exist without energy. Therefore, if I am God, then I AM the original, continuous energy that feeds all things. In me all things would live and move and have their being.

DARKNESS

In my world there would be no darkness at all. Zero darkness. The only apparent blackness would be the absence of light. You could bring a whole box full of darkness into a room and open it up and . . . nothing. Light would jump into the box and dispel all that black-feeling stuff. Nothing in the box would come out, because darkness would be nothing.

Watch what happens, though. As soon as there is an object blocking the light, causing a shadow to fall on our world, people will be tempted to be afraid.

Light, being the greatest symbolic comparison to humanity's creator, is the most obvious outlet of pure energy. Therefore, when the light is taken away, people will feel alone. It will feel as though their Father is not there, and the fear of being abandoned will creep up like a shadow.

However, even in the dead of night, where children's imaginations run wild, all it takes is the tiniest beam of light, the welcome opening of a door, and fear is dispelled. We have all seen it happen on an emotional level. A despairing person finds a real friend, and the sense of hopelessness becomes a memory. As it is in this world, even so it would be in the land that I would create. Light will always be more powerful than darkness.

LIGHT. HEAT. ENERGY.

These three are necessary for plants to grow, and vital for my people and all living beings. Am I boring you? Are you able to grasp the perfection of the world as we know it?

Think about it. Where do people have to go to receive this life-giving energy from the sun? We just have to be somewhere where the light can reach us. And even though it travels in a straight line, the radiance reflects off of objects and around corners. It is free to all. Nobody can say "This sunlight is mine to sell," or "Only certain kinds of people can enjoy this sun."

In my world, as in this one, it would be a universal gift.

ROUND WORLDS

If I Was God . . . All "worlds" would be round. Physics demands it. The very force that holds my people in their homes also shapes their world into something round.

Even the ground that my beings will move across will receive energy from the sun. Hmm. Ground? Maybe I could make a covering for my world.

MUD

Oh, wait a minute. I've got it—this is absolutely genius. I will cover the floor of my beautiful world with mud! Loam! Clay! Soil! Stuff my beings can dig into and move around. And pile up.

That's right. If I Was God . . . I would make mud. I would cover the floor of their homes with earth. And in that earth will grow every kind of plant. Right out of the mud that they move across . . . the very stuff that they will call dirt. Out of that dirt will grow other kinds of life. Life will come bursting out of the mud.

And what will my family have to do to the ground to make other life grow out of it? On their own, plants will produce seeds to grow more of their own kind. And to keep it productive people will save some of the seeds and plant them, and they will grow more plants that produce more seeds! What a concept. Watch it grow. Don't destroy it. Don't exploit it. It will feed them forever if they don't abuse it. Out of my earth life will explode.

The ground that will cover my world, if I am God, will grow plants that creatures can eat.

My beings will eat. What a great idea. Eating. (Yes, I said a great idea. An ingenious, pre-meditated, carefully calculated concept requiring forethought. Not an unguided stroke of chance.) And everything that they need for nourishment will naturally grow out of the mud they walk on.

Oh my God! (That would be me . . . and I would be a Genius . . . If I Was God.)

I've heard a joke that goes something like this:

God and a certain scientist were talking one day, and the man said, "You know, we don't need you anymore."

"Oh? What do you mean?" God asked, a twinkle in Her eye.

"Well, I mean that we can create life on our own. We have the technology. We have discovered what it is in our bodies that makes us alive." he said confidently to The Supreme Being who didn't appear shaken.

"You think you can create human life? Show me."

So the scientist began to gather up amino acids and nutrients. He brought into his laboratory several chemicals and hooked up an electrical generator to create a charge through electrodes feeding into a container shaped like a man. Then his assistants wheeled in a load of clay and started packing it into the anthropoid form.

As they were sculpting God spoke up, "Excuse me. Excuse me."

"What is it?" they asked.

And God quietly replied, "Get your own clay. I made that."

STOMACHS

I can just imagine a bunch of angels chatting with God as he tells them his plan for human beings.

"They will all have stomachs. They will ingest the stuff that grows out of their floor into stomachs."

One of the angels—we'll call him Charlie—can't hold back his confusion. He nudges the more intelligent being beside him and says, "Ummm. What's a stomach?"

The reply: "God only knows. Really! How am I supposed to know? This is all brand new."

Stomachs . . . the things that grow out of the mud will be edible.

Then I would say, "Eat. Be nourished."

The stuff humans will need to eat in order to survive and flourish and grow will naturally rise up out of their floor all around them.

ENRICHING THE MUD

Now this might gross you out a bit, but I think I'll make other creatures that walk on this mud. Big creatures eat the plants, and then they release the stuff that is leftover in their stomachs onto the mud. They will sh_t on the mud, and that will make the plants grow better. Ha.

Who could have thought of that? Poo makes the soil rich. Wow. I am on a roll! What a perfect world I could create. Everything is provided to build healthy, happy human beings.

BEAUTY

In this place they call home, in this house of continuous provision, my beings would be so different from each other and yet so much the same.

I would love to see lots of colour in the skin that wraps around the bodies of my human family. I would make so many epidermis shades. Round faces, square, and slim will all project personality and express what goes on inside these radiant children. Different contours of eyes will all be a window to their souls. How much emotion, how much love, what great determination will shine from within? And I would decorate my people. I would adorn them with cylindrical filaments growing from their epidermis. Long, thin strands would just grow on their own. Hair. They could swirl it. Hair could be stood up on end. Watch people smooth it over and make themselves beautiful.

Beauty? Will they understand the quality present in a thing or person? You've heard it said that beauty is in the eye of the beholder. Please help me out here. What makes a person appreciate some things above others? What is it that gives the "beholder" reason to stand in awe of what something looks like? Would it be valuable to give my family the ability to admire a river flowing off the edge of a cliff, or to experience the wonder of the night sky that is with them at the end of every day? Would that capacity add to one's quality of life? Just looking at scenery, animals, or other created beings inspires us.

What about when the human male sees the whole naked female? If you were God, would you want that to be a big deal? Why should the look of women arouse such delight in men? She may be self-absorbed or angry and malicious. But in front of the camera . . . gorgeous. Who told us to appreciate smooth, soft skin over dry and scaly? I would, if I was God.

GRATITUDE

We are skilfully and awesomely made!

Dr. Paul Brand's work with leprous patients in the poorest countries led to discoveries that have limited the ravaging power of the disease worldwide. When studying the human hand, he came to the conclusion that it is not an anomaly that the body stops functioning, but that it somehow keeps working so long. Something in our mechanics keeps us operational. I would like to suggest that gratitude is the proper response.

Let me ask you this: who can I thank for creating beauty? We honour people who have given us the many great inventions our species has imagined. I would say, however, the female, as an invention, is somewhere just above the male and far beyond anything humans have constructed. Whom shall I commend for this?

The dilemma for the atheist is that when the sense of deep gratitude overwhelms, there is no one to thank.

If I Was God . . . I would not even consider creating any sentient beings without giving them beauty and the appreciation of it. Life would be empty and meaningless without it.

My created beings will have the ability to look at each other and appreciate the individual qualities of each person. Not only will they have beauty, they will also have the comprehension of it. This would be one of my greatest gifts to my family.

Many people say that the universe itself is the greatest miracle. Others exclaim, "The greater miracle is that the human mind can comprehend it." My family will appreciate the stuff around them. They will, in turn, see value in each other.

A SKY FULL OF AIR

Everything in the world that I will build for my family will have its own vibrant quality. And I will have people that are full of gratitude for their world. What a collage. What a kaleidoscope. What a rainbow of skin colour, of personalities, of ideas and beliefs. And I would fill the air with moisture so that when light shines through the air-borne water, another kind of rainbow would appear in the sky.

Again, Charlie, the angel, asks, "What's a sky?"

Thank you, Charlie. First there needs to be a sky. A sky full of air. All my beings will have to do is breathe in the air.

When air passes through the nostrils, making its way into our bodies, expanding and contracting with each breath, our lungs act like a pump for drawing air across tube-like hairs so that oxygen can move into our blood and carbon dioxide is removed. Our cardiovascular system distributes oxygen to needy, oxygen-hungry cells throughout our bodies. All around us there is air giving life and health.

My beings won't have to go get it somewhere, or make it because they will naturally breathe. Wait a minute. I have an idea. Maybe I'll make it impossible to stop breathing. Involuntary activity. Unless one blocks all passages, our bodies will breathe, against our will if necessary. Vital-to-life air will be all around. And the human body will be designed to live on. That is absolutely brilliant! Did I say I was a genius yet? Once or twice?

WATER

Okay, now I'm getting excited. I think I would make water also. Water could wash their bodies, inside and out. Bodies will need water for so many things.

And I think the water should be available to everyone. Where will the water come from?

How will they get this water? I know! I will make it fall from the sky. The air will be all around them. It will be everywhere, and the water that keeps them alive and nourishes them will accumulate in the air and fall from the sky. Water will lie on the ground in pools and lakes and flow everywhere so that everyone can have it. It will be free. Free to everyone.

Again you ask, "What will they have to do to get this water?" It will fall from the sky, I tell you. Don't abuse it. Don't put garbage in it. Protect it. Keep it pure, or this treasure will be spoiled. Don't use it up unnecessarily. Don't contaminate it. It is precious. If we're not careful, we'll have to buy it in bottles someday. Oops.

Taste it. Feel it wash around in your mouth. We need water. Yes, need it. Water makes things grow and washes everything clean. And it mixes with almost everything. It dissolves almost everything. And when they heat the water, it will cook food. When they ingest the food, oh I can taste it now, the water in our stomachs dissolves the food and distributes it where needed in our bodies.

THIS WORLD ... JUST A HAPPY ACCIDENT?

The great atheist Bertrand Russell once said "If there were a God, I think it very unlikely that he would have such an uneasy vanity as to be offended by those who doubt his existence." Okay, Imagine that somehow, this whole world is just a fluke.

Can we honestly think that all of this was created by no one? It just happened?

So . . . . . We boil plants that grow out of the mud in water that falls from the sky . . . over burning wood that grows out of the mud . . . or with flames from gas found under the mud . . . and we ingest the plants into stomachs through a mouth that is a hole in our face . . . we grind up the plants with teeth that naturally grow out of a jaw bone . . . and we digest the plants that grow out of the mud with juices that our stomachs produce . . . and wash it down with the water stored in pockets under the mud and in the lakes and air and rivers and glaciers . . . all of this without Intelligence to guide its creation. Really?

We do all of that . . . two-legged creatures walking upright on the mud . . . and we harness the power of the water that flows in the rivers . . . and on and on and on it goes. Doesn't it strike you as though someone had to put just a little bit of thought into this whole thing we call home?

CHAPTER 9

Blue Marble - Water World

Many elements come together to make this planet inhabitable. One stands at the top of the list, providing countless necessities to create and support life. It is that component which makes the marble blue.

"Water covers 71% of Earth's surface, and is vital for all known forms of life." Wikipedia/Water

---

THERE'S NO PLACE LIKE THAT.

Let's take a walk through an inner-city neighbourhood.

This is no small city, and we ain't in Kansas anymore. We are talking about poverty that the civilised world doesn't ever get close to, unless we're on that cheap holiday. You know, exotic places where you are warned, "Please stay in the tourist areas. Do not venture down any of the back alleys." Well, this story takes us way back, deep into the slums of a third-world country and dangerously close to a massive garbage dump. This is where families are forced to salvage for anything that can be sold in order to live another day.

Let us say that you are here to study what life is like for some of the poorest people in the world. Your mission requires a closer look than you wanted to take. There you meet a young boy heading out for his daily job of scouring. His name is Sammi.

Your interpreter gives him some food and a bottle of water. For that he is willing to stay and talk. She extracts a few bits of information from the child. His dad is gone . . . somewhere. Mom died a while ago. He can't tell you how long he has been without a guardian. Four siblings are still alive. There used to be more of them. Did they die? Just leave? He doesn't know.

Sammi usually spends most of his day at the dump. Fires burn constantly. You aren't about to follow him too far into the carnage because the air is toxic. It is much too dangerous. Some kids melt plastic off of electrical wires to salvage the copper. The ones who do that kind of work are always sick. They don't even know why. A small family is pulling something out of a pail and eating it.

Since this is your first assignment in an area with this kind of horror, you break down. You just can't stand it. The only thing on your mind is bringing Sammi home with you.

"Listen, Sammi, let me tell you about where I live." You say, through the interpreter, "It's a beautiful place. When I go outside in my backyard, the sky is often blue, with white clouds just floating overhead. The air isn't dark and dirty like this. When you breathe really deep, it tastes so sweet inside of you."

The underdeveloped little guy looks up at the grey haze overhead. He is confused. There is a glow revealing the presence of the sun a little to the south. He points.

"Sammi, that's the sun. We can't look directly at it in my town because it is so bright it hurts our eyes."

The boy takes another drink from his bottle of water. He is obviously savouring this. So clean. So delicious. He's only ever had a sample of this magic liquid on three or four very special occasions in his life. The rest of the time his H2O is just a little bit brown.

You want to impress him. "Do you know where we go to get great water like this? You will never guess. Where I live, fresh, clean water falls from the sky."

Uh oh. That was too much for the little guy. "You are lying to me. There's no place like that."

"Listen, Sammi. For thousands of years every place was like that. The water fell right out of the sky, perfectly clean. You didn't have to go anywhere to get it. You could just put a container out, and when it rained, it would fill up. Fresh, life-giving water falling from the sky."

It's just too much of a stretch for Sammi to believe. Your picture of life is too far from the world he knows. Sammi, like much of the world, can't see beyond his present reality.

SOME TECHNICAL INFO WORTH READING

In 2010 about 14% of the world's population (884 million people) did not have access to an improved water source and had to use unprotected wells or springs, canals, lakes, or rivers for their water needs.
http://en.wikipedia.org/wiki/water_supply#global_access_to

The poorest of the inhabitants of planet Earth number well over a billion people. Approximately nine hundred thirty million (of those) people live in middle income countries like China, India, Indonesia and Nigeria. Three hundred seventy million (of the poorest) people live in low income countries.
http://en.wikipedia.org/wiki/the_bottom_billion

These masses of human beings are stuck in some kind of scenario that rolls along like Sammi's existence. That's just the way it is. And the lack of clean water plays a major role in the illnesses that keep these people down.

The very thing that you can't live without—the universal solvent, the stuff you can wash almost anything in—falls from the sky.

You and I grew up swimming in it. I have great memories of getting the garden hose and trying to soak my friends. Life-sustaining liquid falls from the sky and gathers in those breath-taking lakes and rivers. It used to be clean. It used to be free. Now it comes with a few additives, (among other things, a little acid in the rain.)

If I was God . . . I would build a world that had a seemingly endless supply of water.

. . . 96.5% of the planet's water is found in oceans, another .9% is other saline water, **only 2.5% of the Earth's water is freshwater,** and 98.8% of that . . . is in ice and groundwater. http://en.wikipedia.org/wiki/Lakes

Less than 0.3% of all freshwater is in rivers, lakes and the atmosphere.

So much water! And only 3/1000's of the fresh water (that is 0.3% of the 2.5%) is in lakes and rivers and the atmosphere. Let me put this into perspective for you. Try to picture in your mind all of the world's freshwater lakes and rivers and all of the moisture in the atmosphere. Massive amounts of freshwater is lying in lakes and flowing along river-beds. And that is only 0.3% of the fresh water on planet Earth.

OKAY. FURTHER PERSPECTIVE. LET'S PLAY A GAME.

Pretend you want to gather up all of the water from the lakes and rivers on the globe. (I don't know why you like doing things like this, but you do.) However, you only have ten five-gallon pails. So you start at Lake Titicaca on the border of Peru and Bolivia – or perhaps on the shore of Great Slave Lake in Northern Canada, or maybe the little pond nearest to your house – with your ten pails. How many times do you think you would have to fill those pails to empty every lake and river in the world? How many trips will you have to make? Are you with me?

You go to every lake and river and remove ten pails at a time until all bodies of fresh water are empty. So much water. Imagine standing on the shorelines of the Great Lakes with ten pails.

At the same time, I'm going to assemble a team of people to go to all of the salt-water seas and oceans with a bunch of pails. How many pails would I need to fill so that every time you fill your ten pails I fill mine and we empty the lakes and the oceans with an equal numbers of trips? Every time you fill your ten containers I will have to draw out enough pails to cover two American football fields. Approximately 115,000 pails.

Count it. Your ten, my two football fields, your ten, my two football fields, your ten pails . . . and we end at the same time. And you thought that you had a lot of drawing to do. Unfathomable amounts of water.

Wikipedia, "The majority of lakes on Earth are fresh water, and most lie in the Northern Hemisphere at higher latitude. Canada . . . has an estimated 31,752 lakes larger than 3 km² (2 miles²) and an unknown total number of lakes, but is estimated to be at least 2 million."

Again, that's a lot of water.

I'M SORRY Sammi, you thought that there was no place like that. There is. It is where we all live. Provision has been made for everyone. The lack of fresh water supply is caused by the lack of infrastructure and planning. That's why our children do without and suffer from the resultant disease. As we speak, every country in the world could produce enough food to feed their own people. The shortage happens when we grow cash crops and sell them to the highest bidder. That's when our own children go hungry.

The home that I would build might be just as vulnerable as this one. I think I would have to leave it up to my family to protect their home. Was it wise to give that responsibility to humans? Could I make beings and not leave some things up to them? Could I force them to protect the world I made?

I'M SORRY that the leaders of countries all over the world won't step up and protect a billion people like yourself.

I'M SORRY that we, in the developed world, haven't figured out how to help you either.

Let me apologize for all of us, Sammi. Only a few are responding to the needs you have. The rest of us are helping a little when we can and trying to make our way within our own societies.

If I Was God . . . my most important commandment would be to love the people around you and abroad (your neighbour) as much as you love yourself.

If I Was God, I would . . . I would . . . I don't know what I would do. The world is a dangerous place. I really don't have a solution. I would love my children. I would want them to flourish. Multiply. Fill the Earth. Not too full. I would say, "Spread out a little. Live simply. Share. Take care of each other. Don't be greedy."

But it would have to be their choice.

If I Was God . . . I would invent INVENTORS.

I would create a professor in Calgary, Alberta who would, in turn, design a sand-filled water purification system and almost singlehandedly interrupt the epidemic of stomach/diarrheal disease in third-world countries where it is used.

Environmental Engineer David Manz - link http://www.manzwater-info.ca

If I Was God . . . I would give Stephen Lewis, Companion of the Order of Canada, so much compassion and courage to speak about the hardships others are facing.

"The Stephen Lewis Foundation (SLF) works with community-level organizations which are turning the tide of HIV/AIDS in Africa by providing care and support to women, orphaned children, grandmothers and people living with HIV and AIDS. Since 2003, we (SLF) have funded over 700 initiatives, partnering with 300 community-based organizations in the 15 African countries hardest hit by the pandemic."

http://www.stephenlewisfoundation.org/

My beings will be inquisitive. Some of them will not rest until they discover new territories in their world. Some will take stuff apart and study the mechanics and then make things work better. Others will spend a whole lifetime trying to create new ways of accomplishing what needs to be done to survive and flourish.

A few will make great personal sacrifices to ensure others are safe and warm, fed, healed, happy, and not lonely anymore.

What beautiful creatures these humans can be. What a glorious world we have to live in.

What love surrounds us. So much potential.

CHAPTER 10

Weakness and Need

The world is grateful to Archbishop Emeritus Desmond Tutu for introducing us to Ubuntu: "We can only be who we are because of what all of humanity is." He taught us that no one can be human all alone. To be truly human is dependent upon interaction, unity, and community. All dehumanizing action diminishes the perpetrator as it does the victim.

My Family, "Ubuntu" - "I am what I am because of who we all are."
https://tutufoundationuk.org/ubuntu.php

If I Was God . . . I would insist that my people are built with needs. That's right. My people would not be self-sufficient. They wouldn't be able to thrive without help and assistance from somewhere outside of themselves. I would provide them with needs.

Members of my humanity would cease to exist if cut off from sunlight, water, food, or some combination of a host of necessities mysteriously required if one is to live "naturally" on Earth.

If I Was God . . . my kids would need each other. In my universe it will be a fact that "the absence of love can kill you," and it will be absolute genius. Being dependent upon others is not a deficiency. It is not something that makes us less powerful or weak. What strength it is to give in, to surrender one's heart to one's need for another person.

My people's great distinction will be an apparent weakness. It will not be good for anyone to be alone. Loneliness will drive my family to be with one another. In my world, being strong enough to be alone without companionship will be a deficiency.

The need to be one with others will be a source of power for life. But even that will not be safe. To have a great need for others will also create danger. The very ability to be vulnerable is to open up to the possibility of injury. Vulnerability . . . makes you vulnerable.

Is it possible to be in need of another person's care without surrendering your well-being to that person? In relationships we relinquish some portion of control. Will he or she provide the care I desire, or withhold it?

People ask why God made us so breakable. Consider this: skin is easily cut and bruised. If our outer layer was like armour, we could crash around and not be hurt. Injury would be rare. However, if our skin was thick, then how would we enjoy the gentle touch? The caress would be meaningless. Choosing to build a wall of protection inherently eliminates the opportunity for close encounters of the intimate kind. And intimacy is not always sexual. So much pleasure resonates in the love-fest of unguarded mutual appreciation.

The obvious spin-off from this train of thought is in the emotional level. Build a wall for protection and you will keep people out. In so doing, you eliminate the risk of being "cut" in the fleshy area of your heart, and the opportunity for a soul-mate to hold that tender heart in theirs is lost. A tragedy. Life without love.

We are all vulnerable the moment we are born. But there is more to it than that.

People ask, "Where was God when tragedy struck?" However, where are the cries demanding to know, "Who built us with so much capacity for pleasure?"

I wonder, how it is that the majority of our so-called sins are merely an over-indulgence in God-given pleasures? It seems to boil down to the simple fact that what we have been given is so undeniably good that we can't seem to control our lust for more.

If I Was God . . . when that so-called superstar, diva, songwriter and performer Grace Wonder-Star showed up on my front porch after her death by overdose, I would absolutely melt in my love for her. I would have to remind myself that I made her. Such a beauty.

But when she saw me, when she looked into my eyes . . . If I Was God . . . she would cry like the little girl that was buried deep inside. She would weep for days. All the pain that drove her from self-destruction to rehab and back, all the times she wished she could have "gotten it together," would come pouring out. Through seemingly endless dives into darkness, again and again, she was literally destroying herself.

Finally she would say, "I am so sorry. I should have—" And then she would proceed to tell me all about how she was hurt.

And I would reply, "I know."

She would try to make me believe that she had done everything she could. "I wanted to . . . I really wanted to. All of my friends were just partying and—"

"Oh. So it wasn't really you making those bad decisions?" I would have to interject.

She would fall into my arms. And the crying would begin again. This talented beauty would finally allow me to break down the walls that kept us apart.

I would ask, "Wasn't it you who sang that song . . . .

Carry Me, Love Me
Please Be Proud of Me
I Am So Broken
Words Go Unspoken
Aching Inside

Oh How I've Cried!

What were you trying to say?

Stay Right Here
I'm So Full of Fear
Open My Heart
I Need a New Start
I Can't Be Alone
I Need a Home."

She would reply, "It was just a song."

"Really? Just a song? I felt your pain when you sang it on stage. You despised your fans for not hearing the desperation. I heard the cry of your heart. I felt the longing for someone to understand that all of the so-called romance in your life was not what you wanted. I was there when you threw the glass at the mirror in your hotel room." Then I would remind her of all the times I had tried to get through to her.

At this point, Grace would look at me, then drop her view to our feet.

"What is it, Grace?"

She would turn and walk away. "I can't take this anymore."

Without another word, she would slowly descend the stairs and cross the lawn. Suddenly, the vibrant colours of the forest before her turn to grey. No leaves adorn the trees, and only dust surrounds her footsteps where once the forest floor was alive with colour. Just like so many times when she chose darkness over light. Then she would disappear as death enveloped her.

Sometime later, though, Grace would step back out of the blackness. No longer young and beautiful, her retreat into the void had sucked the life out of her. Grace was becoming less and less human as she gave in to despair. Slowly she would make her way across my lawn and back up the stairs, where she would find me watching for her and aching to take her back.

"Oh. It is so good to see you. I thought you were gone for good! Hey, everybody. Grace is back! Get out the best wine. I've been saving some Mexican food for you, Grace. We had some new arrivals. They are starting to prepare a fiesta we'll never forget."

"I can't go to your party. I never wanted to be with you. I am not fit to be a guest in your house."

"Grace. Look at me. I know your heart better than you do."

"It doesn't matter. I've screwed up. It's over. I know the rules. I just wanted to say goodbye."

"I love you, Grace."

"I love you too."

Silence. I would wait for her to think about what she had said. Finally, she would speak. "I thought you had left me alone. I thought I had crossed a line and you would never forgive me."

"I love you, Grace."

"I know. I love you too. I love everything about you. I love most of all how you loved me enough to keep working on me. You never let me feel good about running away. You always pressed me to overcome my anger towards life. I was so self-centered."

"Yes, you were. But I was always with you."

"Yeah. I guess I knew you were."

"Do you remember when you wrote:

I'm Right Here

Why Can't You See Me?

You're Not Alone

I've Been Here All Along."

"Oh, God. I remember writing that as though it was you speaking. It was like you were sitting there at the kitchen table with me."

"I was."

"I let it all slip away. Everything that you gave me. It was right there in front of me. I really wanted—"

And I would interrupt again. "I know you did."

"I'm so sorry."

I would repeat the mantra one more time. "I know."

"What am I going to do now?"

"Now? Do you want to learn? You will find that here there is time to accept who you are. You're not famous here, you know. You're just that little girl trying to be a princess. You've got a lot of starting over to do. You are also the young woman who believed in all of that worship your fans laid on you. You have to let that go."

"They really loved me, didn't they?"

I would have to agree with her. "Yes they did, in a shallow sort of way. But nobody is built for that kind of adoration. You might have been okay if you hadn't inhaled."

"Inhaled?" She would look at me. "What?" Her sobs begin again. Laughing. Crying.

"Yes. You inhaled." At this point I wouldn't be able to help myself, but would burst into deep belly laughs. Healing guffaws would come pouring out. And she would look confused again, just for a moment. We would both break into hilarious laughter. Tears flowing as the tension falls away. Then Grace would really break down, and her weeping would wash away a little more of the pain that drove her to her death. While wiping away her tears, I would see skin smoothing out, wrinkles disappearing. Grace's youth returning.

Soon I would have to be serious again. "You inhaled. You took it all in. You believed the lies. You believed that you were some kind of goddess. Well, mostly you wanted to believe that you were. And yet, somehow you are that princess. You are a radiant wonder of a human being. You are beautiful. But really, you're no better than anyone else. Did you make yourself that way?"

"No. I didn't want to be worshipped!" She would say staring angrily at me.

"Yes you did."

"No I didn't. I couldn't help it. They kept raising me higher."

"Yes. Yes you did. You could have asked for help, sweetheart."

Silence. "It was so real."

"You wanted it to be real."

"How am I ever going to get it right? Obviously I can't fix anything now. It's over. I screwed up all of that opportunity. I'm so stupid."

"It won't help to feel sorry for yourself. Most humans are stupid to some degree. You can't fix the past. But it is exactly that. It is past. You have left a legacy of pain behind you. You say that your friends were pushing you deeper. You influenced a lot of them, too. You can't fix that now."

Grace's heart would begin to break as she finally allowed herself to think about someone else's well-being. "Is Sally going to be all right?"

"I don't know. She might be able to find the courage to go to rehab again. I'm talking to her, but . . . I don't know."

"What do you mean? You really don't know?"

"I know what she's thinking. I know what she wants to do. Will she do it? I don't know. But I will help her if she lets me."

"I'm so sorry."

"I know."

"Please help her."

"I'm standing beside her right now. If she asks for help, she will find the courage."

"Why didn't I just appreciate everything I had?"

And then the God of the whole universe, namely me . . . If I Was God . . . would say, "Well now. That's a really good question. I'm going to give you a whole lot of time to answer a whole lot of questions. But you're here now. Do you understand? You are here . . . right now. You came back, and I will never forsake you. My mercy is going to celebrate over everybody's idea of judgement. How far does my mercy extend? Forever! If you are willing to judge yourself honestly and stay with us, you will never have to go back into the dark regions again. A lot of poison lingers in your system. It has to be removed, and there is no one left to blame. But you have to believe that here, the judge and jury are on your side. Nobody wants you to fail here. Do you want to learn? Are you willing to accept who you have been? It is going to be very painful. But I will wipe away all of your tears."

That's what I would say . . . If I Was God.

If I Was God . . . I would wrestle with how to offer the benefits that come with being people who have needs while allowing the risk of abuse. Would it be worth the risk? What if my people use the needs of others only to take advantage?

If I Was God . . . I would be so upset with how people hurt each other. And with how they hurt themselves. I think I would cry a lot . . . If I Was God. Oh, but I would also let them know that I created them so that I would have someone. I would want to be with someone, much the same way people don't want to be alone.

If I Was God . . . would I be in need? How could I have needs? Could I be God and lack anything? Maybe my desire for a special someone would not be springing from a position of need.

Maybe . . . If I Was God . . . my desire for others would come from the sheer joy of sharing. Do you have a god? Is your god filled with joy? Is your god thrilled at the sight of you? If not, maybe you should look for a new one.

I might want someone to enjoy my created things with me. What do you think? Is it possible for God to be with someone as they experience life? Can you conceive of God wanting to spend time with a human being? Should a human be able to spend time with God?

If I Was God . . . I would want everybody to share life with me.

Life, Love, Joy, Food
Extreme Adventure, Friends
Love, Puppies, Babies, Rock and Roll
Peace, Sports, the Arts
Mountains, Hiking, Happiness
Music - Music - Music
Nature and Love.

Did I mention Love?

Would that be so strange, to think that God would want to share life with you? Should believing that be more difficult than it is to have faith in the love you feel so deep inside, yet cannot examine or dissect?

CHAPTER 11

—

Wonder

Earth's environment carries the fundamental ingredients required to build fantasy and fairy tale. Right here, right now, our backyards are bristling with activity.

If I Was God . . . I would create the capacity for amazement in the hearts of my children. And I would build into every single person a fascination for mystery. But come with me to an institutional setting where emotions and psyche have been damaged. Watch the individual reactions to a great thunderstorm. A healthy person will go to the window and exclaim, "Hey, look at this!" Those who are broken on the inside don't bother to get up. The wonder of life has died.

I know . . . If I Was God . . . that I would cry a lot. Wouldn't you? Wonder requires joy. But real happiness is a risk.

If I Was God . . . I would know that human psyche needs to have hope. When a person is healthy, she reaches out to others, she opens herself up to receive from others, and that is dangerous. Soft hearts can be broken. But where does hope come from in our man-made world of concrete, pavement, mortgages, and the constant pressure to perform.

Come sit with me at a campsite. A fire is burning. We're sipping a fine red Malbec wine from Argentina. We have just cooked over the open fire. Before heading out with the camping trailer, I purchased kiln-dried ends from a wood-moulding manufacturer in Calgary, Alberta. Then we drove into Kananaskis Country.

I look around and there, standing straight up and rising out of the mud, are trees. Just standing there, thirty feet tall. Fifty feet. Straight up. The wind is blowing, they bend and sway, but they don't fall.

Wood has just a few uses. As trees it provides homes for birds, animals, and insects. Trees give shade and hold moisture in the ground while removing carbon dioxide from the air. These pulpy plants eat harmful carbon dioxide and produce healthy air for us to breathe. Forests are the lungs of our sister Earth. What a cool idea!

If I was God . . . I hope I would be smart enough to invent trees.

When trees are harvested, we can use the wood for fuel: firewood, charcoal, chips, pellets, and sawdust. Have you ever heard of the skill of carpentry? Of course you have. Wood is the basic building block in home construction, floors, walls, roofing, cabinetry, stairs, windows, doors, furniture, and on and on.

Wood derivatives are found in a million products that include cellulose, terpenes, and rosin. Varnish that preserves wood is often made up of wood extracts. Adhesives that glue wood together can be made from trees. Soap to wash the wood table, paper to order the table from the furniture store, the pencil used to draw the original design for the table, the printing ink that photocopies the order form, and the seal on the lawyer's document proving you own the two-hundred-year-old antique can be made from trees.

Rosin is also used in pharmaceutical capsules and film to coat tablets.

A vast number of musical instruments are manufactured with wood that enhances and reverberates the sound: woodwind instruments, stringed, percussion, and so on. In carving, from ancient artifacts to First Nations totem poles depicting family history, to modern architecture, the use of wood has shaped our past and is carved into our future. Can we go anywhere to get away from our dependence upon wood products?

And here I sit, burning wood beside a wooden picnic table, marvelling at a small stand of trees on the edge of a mountain range more than four-hundred miles wide in some places, that begins in Alaska to the north and runs south through Alberta and British Columbia in Canada, through the western United States and into Mexico. Then they seem to dip into the ocean, only to rise again in South America as the Andes Mountains, where they continue right down through Argentina, where the Malbec grape is grown and turned into wine in an oak barrel. Then it is shipped in boxes on wooden skids, displayed on wooden shelves in the store, and poured into my glass in this stand of trees.

Would I ever love to be the guy, the God, who invented the tree. There they stand, whispering in the wind, and I am struck by their beauty. The use of this plant has shaped our modern world. Without missing a beat, it is also so aesthetically pleasing that artists and photographers capture it for viewing inside our metallic and concrete structures. Engineers design buildings with trees rising up through the ceiling and into the next storey.

I am in awe. I am grateful. I could be a tree-hugger.

Is astonishment the correct response to nature? Should it blow your mind? Let it. Be amazed. This gig called life that we find ourselves in is beyond what anyone has been able to prepare us for.

If I Was God . . . I would want my children to be captivated every day. Not everybody can be a scientist and study the depth of design built into every speck of creation, but life is vibrating all around us.

I would ask, "Are you amazed by my four-legged creations?"

If I Was God . . . I would have to say, "Look at that white-tailed deer. I made that. She's perfect." And puppies? Seriously. How would anyone be unable to recognize my extreme, God-sized fun when they see a puppy?

Can we revisit two of the marvels of creation already discussed? Ponder the sun again for just a moment. Consider that unfathomable explosion of energy so far away in space. So far away that it is impossible to travel to this ball of fire . . . not possible with the technology we have achieved so far. It is so hot that no one could get close to it without bursting into flame—even if we could make the journey.

Yet it is so perfectly distanced from our home, from this planet that has been built for us, situated with undeniable precision. People lie naked in the gentle rays, and beautiful skin soaks it in. Life-giving energy pouring into us from 93,000,000 miles away.

Not close enough to burn, not so far away as to freeze. Perfectly positioned for someone to enjoy: the rising and the setting and the midday heat of the sun.

If I was God . . . every square centimetre of my world would explode with wonder.

And light. Changing every moment, revealing colour . . . illuminating beauty for my family, for my people, for humans to appreciate.

And pure, clean water. What a miracle. Splashing. Soaking. Floating. Washing. Drinking. Water washing, cleansing my people from the inside out. And then — you're going to love this — peeing it back out as it removes the impurities from inside this body that I have created. Come on. You know who thought of that, don't you?

If I was God . . . I would say, "I did. That was my idea. Don't you think it's the coolest thing ever?"

Ha. Peeing. I'm a genius. I would be reminded of the first day that I looked upon my created ones and said they are very good. Wow. And Adam saw Eve for the very first time and said . . . well, that's personal. You will have to ask him yourself one day. Anyway. Imagine his surprise when he woke up from that apparent operation and saw her. I would want to have a Someone— perhaps a whole world of Someones to be in awe of each other.

If I was God . . . I would want to create someone like me. Someone above the animals. To find pleasure in Creation. To share all things with me.

Every time a person would "get it," every time someone would have eyes to see and ears to hear what I have prepared for those who "get me," for those who love me, I would experience that great joy all over again. What moments we would share. A life of meaning would be available. What opportunity there would be to experience all that is exploding around us every day.

Humanity. Creation's crowning achievement. So much possibility.

Do you know who you are?

This is a story about someone who had a child at the age of sixteen. She became a parent at that age. The offspring is now fourteen. His aunt has taken care of him for the last six years. That child has a lot to deal with. Mom couldn't be what he needed her to be. Now his aunt can't handle him anymore. His so-called dad was gone before he was born. It's an all-too-familiar story.

Does this fourteen-year-old feel wanted? Should he? He might become an angry man. Or he could turn it on himself. Will he want to hurt himself? Or others? Perhaps he'll do the same thing his father did.

He asks himself, "Am I the result of an evening of indiscretion? Is there any purpose for my life?"

But whatever impulses were the motivation of the act that spawned him, no matter what circumstances led to him living somewhere other than with his mother, regardless of the emotional baggage he carries and will have to deal with in order to find some sort of normal existence . . . he is still human.

The person who looks out from behind his eyes works in intimate partnership with the most sophisticated computer ever designed: the human brain.

He also captains (when it is not bullying him) an unparalleled network of emotion and compassion, intuition and forethought . . . and much, much more. He is #1 in the hierarchy of created beings—top of the food chain, if you will. In spite of his challenges—no, maybe because of his undesirable circumstances—he may rise to meet the demons that haunt him. He just might go on to achieve things that I never dreamed of for myself. Or he may become a caring individual who understands the needs of others because he himself has been there. Perhaps, at the right time, he'll show kindness to someone else at a pivotal moment, and that act of compassion, that understanding, will send another person on her journey to a more-than-average existence.

However big or small his accomplishments may be, he could still be one of the good ones. He could become an important influence to a few people. His laughter and frustration will help shape and mould the thoughts and aspirations of another.

No matter what he does, whether he realizes it or not, he is a magnificent creature. A walking, talking miracle of a thing.

We stand in awe . . . a master creation/invention.

When his mother shows up at my door, I have only love for her. I look at her and see beauty. What a brilliant creation. Will I be angry with her? Should she be afraid of me? If I am God, then I am the one who conceived the idea of "her" in the first place.

So many people have so much stuff going on inside; more than they are willing to deal with.

If I Was God . . . my mercy and my desire to forgive would celebrate over judgement. Many would argue that I am too soft. The character played by John Travolta in the movie *Swordfish* said, "Do not mistake my kindness for weakness." Too soft? If I Was God . . . I would not be soft. But I would be love.

There are those who are admiring of their own achievements. I applaud them. Life was hard, but some rose above the obstacles. However, as soon as a person begins to view himself above another and then freaks out over a flaw, a splinter in a weaker person's eye, right then a log begins to grow in his. Vision becomes blurred. Pride begins to erode the qualities that fostered achievement.

At that point, the courage and inherent humility of one who rose above loses its strength. Purposes change, and somehow all of those accomplishments take on an air of falsehood. His present attitude convinces others that there was self-serving all along. Suddenly, the man who is judging is now being scrutinized in the same way he judges others. He was honourable back then. But the very way he views others now condemns him.

"Remove the log from your own eye and you will see clearly enough take the speck out of your sister's eye." -Jesus

Take a long look at a teenager. Focus on the beauty of the construction. Nothing in the universe holds more promise. Just try and build one of those units. The human body? The power of the mind? The emotional depth? The capacity for love? Yet our teens are struggling. Where there is no vision for life, they perish and meaningful hope for the future is crushed within them.

Do you know who you are? Can you see the people in your life for who they really are? Beauty is in your eye if you choose to behold it.

CHAPTER 12

Beauty, Pleasure, and Gratitude

"Beauty is a manifestation of secret natural laws, which otherwise would be hidden from us forever." -Johann Wolfgang von Goethe

"Nothing would be more tiresome than eating and drinking if God had not made them a pleasure as well as a necessity." -Voltaire

"Gratitude is a cure for a host of ailments and it brings no negative side effects. However, it can be the hardest pill to swallow by the very persons who are most concerned with their own well-being." -Gerry Bast

Every day of our life we are inundated with beauty. Bombarded. It is so common, we have become numb to it. Let me start with something that can be overwhelming beauty to the beholder: a desk. You didn't see that coming, did you? A desk. Overwhelming beauty.

If you take the perspective of children in third-world countries who ache to be in school, a classroom full of old, donated students' desks are about as delicious a sight as can be imagined. You might say that it is not the desk they are seeing but the dream. Exactly. A deep sense that the world is now at his or her fingertips fills that child's emotions. When she gets to sit in it, it compares to you walking into the corner office for the first time . . . with your name on the door.

On a level of aesthetics, that dented and worn student's desk with the metal tube attaching the aged wooden seat . . . . To the child, nothing is more pleasing. With regards to the practical, it compares to a shiny new tractor pulling into the lane after its long awaited purchase.

Now let's bring this process back to a definition of beauty that we can better relate to. I have refinished a few antique desks. Let me tell you about aged mahogany when it is properly sanded, lovingly stained, and lacquered, creating a rich satin sheen. If you can appreciate wood products, it makes you want to stroke them like the neck of a fine horse.

A few years back we did a makeover of the main floor of our home. We painted our walls a deep green in the living/dining area and installed knotty walnut flooring that stretched from the breakfast bar to the fireplace. Mixing the green with white paint for the hallway gave it the same tone and half the depth of colour. On the two walls framing the antique walnut dining table we had refinished, we installed white tongue and groove wainscoting that was antiqued to reveal a dark stain beneath aged white lacquer. From a one-hundred-year-old "pound piano" (so-named because somewhere around 1900 AD, after arriving in North America on a ship from England, it would have sold for one British Pound) from the keyboard lid, I built a flower box and hung it beside the antique walnut table against the white wood. Ivy hanging over the box draped in front of the white. And then, to round it all off, we took a photo of the room, transferred it onto an older-looking paper, mounted it in a gilded picture frame, and hung it on the deep olive-green wall that was actually in the photo above the wainscoting beside the table. Beauty? Absolutely surrounded by it like a well-planned ambush. That is where we live.

These are everyday influences in our mundane lives. But then to break the monotony of our own creative artistry, we head into the mountains. After an hour of driving along some magnificent highway to heaven through Kananaskis Country, my face begins to ache from smiling for so long. It reminds me of having to put on a face while standing in a receiving line for an hour after a wedding. We are overwhelmed by the majesty of the Rocky Mountains. It fills our souls with the wonder that has drawn millions of tourists to the area over the years.

On any given morning, I crawl out of bed and down the stairs to the kitchen described above. If I'm not having a shower that day in my ensuite bathroom, I wash my hyper-sensitive scalp in the kitchen sink because I don't want to bend into the tub to do it anymore. I use this great Nioxin shampoo every day. It is so rich and concentrated, one half litre lasts me a year. Of course, I don't have that much hair. It feels so good to scrub a little.

By the time I'm done my scalp and perusing the morning headlines, it's time to pour the boiling water into the French press and brew some of the best coffee this side of the Rockies and beyond. Jill and I sit with an inspirational book and read to one another before facing the day. My own brewed coffee, with a double portion of 18% cream and a quarter teaspoon of sugar, kick-starts the day with great pleasure. (Yeah, my belly could do without the cream and sugar, but it is so good that way.)

In comfortable shoes, I walk into my attached garage and drive in a well-tuned vehicle with air conditioning and a stereo. We adjust the volume to set the mood, or Jill reads aloud— inspiration - challenge - assurance - hope - courage to face the day—and it takes our minds off of city traffic. The drive to work is a pleasure compared to some of the vehicles I have had to pilot/manoeuvre/wrestle into submission.

At work my office chair, my shoes, clothing, climate control, and food (with Tim Horton's coffee) is made more enjoyable by the people I choose to work with: my family. Conversation, laughter, and respect fill some part of every day.

At home in the evening I sit with Jill and a glass of wine. Then I experience her great cooking. She loves to make every meal an event, often with candlelight, and even when Guy is with us. We have had the great fortune of having Guy Campeau board with us on week days while he teaches in Calgary at The Third Academy, a school for kids with special needs. Throughout the meal, Monsieur Campeau regales us with stories. Events from our past are relived, until we realize we need to actually get up from the table before we drink too much or run out of time to do "what needs to be done" that evening.

These are everyday events! What about all of the pleasures we only enjoy occasionally? Concerts, sports events, SEX, friendship, movies, meals over an open fire, travel, camping... the list goes on and on. Again, we are absolutely inundated with pleasure like a well-planned ambush.

We live and breathe beauty. Pleasure accompanies us through our days, but are we immune to it? Rather, are we so accustomed to the quality of life permeating every moment that we become the cliché: "We don't know what we've got 'til it's gone"? The very things we used to long for are now all around us, and the sense of gratitude that formerly accompanied these experiences is diminished or forgotten entirely.

Gratitude. I haven't studied this, but it may be a medical fact that physical health is enhanced by being grateful. It is possibly the best weapon we can wield against the ravages of anxiety. (Okay, I just went online—it is well-known.) Within our bodies, oxytocin is released as we experience an appreciation for life, for others, and for gifts received. There is also the exhilaration we feel as we show gratitude, as we express appreciation, and when we take time to help someone else.

If I Was God . . . If I was the one who built this world for you, I would know that the "command" to offer up gratitude to one's Creator would not be selfish on my part. I would recommend some form of worship of me; I would suggest a thankful heart. I would build into my kids' psyche the extreme pleasure of making someone else feel good about themselves. What an ingenious concept. When we see the good in others, when we express what we see, when we stop navel-gazing and let go of our selfish thoughts, we enhance our own lives and the lives of others physically, emotionally and spiritually.

Genius? I would dare to say that gratitude has to be one of the top ten inventions ever!

———

CHAPTER 13

Now You Know What I Would Do

Is your God neatly packaged in an easy-to-understand format? Do you have a convenient explanation for every situation that arises? Are you sure that "that God" is your Creator? Or has he been tampered with and manipulated until we are no longer dealing with deity?

I quite expect that if you are still working your way through this book, you have a pretty good picture of where I stand on the questions we have asked.

"Is there Someone out there?" You know that I am sure there is.

"Is the universe friendly?" I say yes. Our world is filled with nourishment. Everywhere and in every way LIFE is being poured into us and into all living things. Whatever we do to her, Nature struggles to revive and provide for us.

"Is planet Earth a safe place to live?" We hear reports of the danger every day. Read a newspaper, check out any internet news site. Our world is not safe.

"But is it good?" Are you breathing? If so, that would mean something good is happening to you right now. The energy that sustains you is being generated in your body as we speak. For as long as humans have had the ability to process thought, we have pondered and formally researched the million, trillion phenomena we understand to be Nature. The everyday, mundane activity of our environment is the all-too-common nurturing of all living things. Nature, at every turn is working to sustain us.

"How can a good God allow such pain?" Within the few short pages presented here, we have only had an elementary discussion on that topic. I don't know if anyone will ever understand all that went into the decision to include the possibility that humanity could fall into so much misery. I am left to hope that it will make sense someday. And for me, I must believe that whatever being had the ability to create planet Earth also had the forethought, and thus a plan to fulfill Her good purpose. No longer do I have the luxury of holding to one part of the equation of a supreme intelligence and ignoring the other. Supreme - all powerful. Intelligence - having "the Smarts". I cannot hold to power and simultaneously believe that She has been caught by surprise by our fallibility. God could not be heard to be saying, "Oops! I didn't see that coming!" I deliberately choose to trust that He/She is not overwhelmed by the ever present deficiency in our human condition.

"What is God like?" In these discussions, notably without your permission, I have affirmed faith in the Judeo-Christian account of creation, history, incarnation of the Son of God, and His death and resurrection. I have tried to introduce you to a God who is more in agreement with the Biblical accounts of the life of Jesus than what we have heard in a long, long time. If Jesus and His Father are one, as the scripture says they are, then we should expect God to be right there saying, with Jesus, "I forgive them, for they do not know what they are doing." Jesus would not have to die to protect humanity from the wrath of his Father.

And . . . If There is a God, then we would be wise to expect Him to be free from human fears and anger. God cannot be 'less of a man' than we. He cannot be so easily offended as many of us are.

"Are we alone while a god watches us from afar?" There has been some form of evolution of mankind. We find accounts of a barbaric human race in every ancient historical record. If we were ever like the animals, it goes without saying that we were not recording anything at that juncture of our history. But the most ancient accounts point to a time when we were more basic than we are now. We have evolved throughout our known history. Beyond that, I must concede, someone has guided us throughout our growth. Every indigenous group has stories of that great someone, who has been interacting with humanity.

I can't say much about other religions, because I have not studied their claims. And I have no need to dispute their stance on God. If He or She is intelligent enough to create all of this, once again, we must concede Her ability to communicate with every single creature She chooses to. I also understand that many good and honest people disagree wholeheartedly with my beliefs. God has not felt the need to ask me for some kind of clearance as to whom He might seek out for a parley. Any honest seeker must admit to being certifiably misinformed in some areas of his or her faith, in the same way I must be. And yet I sense His presence, active, challenging, and most assuredly offering vision and hope. God communicates with and comforts even the likes of me.

At this moment a Jewish woman bows her head at the great Wailing Wall in Jerusalem; she is wearing a prayer shawl. For all of known history, only males wore it to approach their God. She isn't just being rebellious. She longs for contact.

When Malala Yousafzai, Pakistani activist for female education and the youngest-ever Nobel Prize laureate, defies the rules regulating women's activities and advocates for the opportunity for girls to receive an education, she prays for courage, and with many others in her great country, she addresses the God of Abraham out of a sincere heart.

A young Islamic man kneels on his mat to pray. He cries "Allah bring us peace." Not all Muslims despise the so-called infidels. For some, their hatred is directed towards the violence pouring out of opposing religions and they pray with sincerity for all parties to seek Shalom.

In any number of countries, a Christian sways to the music in a modern church. Tears begin to flow, and she prays to be more like Jesus.

People of no religious affiliation work tirelessly for a better world and a cooperative humanity.

Are all religions the same? Certainly not. Is any religion as good as another? There are wide differences and varying purposes. Can a person find God in any religion? M. Scott Peck, who claims to have found God in Zen Buddhism, suggested that alcoholism could lead you to the one Creator. So, he seems to suggest that one can find God in any religion. A billion sincere hearts around the world, with a myriad of opposing images of God in mind, humble themselves, hoping that whoever is listening will give them an audience.

But out there, beyond our physical perception, do all but a few voices dissipate, unheard, into the great empty void? That thought defies the whole notion of a good God. At present there is a trend toward atheism. And that in itself is a form of religion, with beliefs that adherents must hold to. But the vast majority of us continue to have faith in someone who is responsible for Creation and active in daily life. Down through history we have embraced that hope, and hope will not be quenched.

If I was the God who had started all of this, would I turn down the volume and ignore the prayers that didn't follow proper protocol? After going to the trouble of making a habitation for such a diverse bunch of bipeds, should we not expect the creator would have some sort of plan for what to do with us? If God is so smart as to design us in the first place, I suspect that She might be just a little above our programs for reaching Her.

It is easy to imagine that God is watching us like an instructor who has presented his students with a difficult question; in this case, the mystery of life itself. Is He deliberately allowing the struggle we find ourselves in?

I expect that many adherents to other faiths are conversing with him at this very moment. If you don't like it, you can take it up with Him. When a person with an honest heart prays to that great someone, if that someone is truly great, He or She will acknowledge. And let me say this in the most respectful way possible. God will not be under any obligation to refer to our

THREE SUBTLE BASICS
FOUR SPIRITUAL LAWS
FIVE COSMIC ELEMENTS
SIX PATHS TO GOD
FOUR PATHS TO GOD
NINE STEPS TO NIRVANA
PATH OF RETURN
Or THE RULES OF KARMA

I sincerely hope that the-God-of-all-there-is listens to all hearts as much as He hears mine, regardless of cultural influence.

As for my experience, I have been privileged to hear and understand the very good news . . .

That we are not alone,
That God Himself descended, in human form, to live among us and
That because we couldn't stand to have Him live on a level so far above ours,
That we killed Him to shield ourselves from His revealing light,
That though He died, Death could not hold Him because I know
That life cannot die, and I believe
That death does not have the last say.

"All I am doing is to ask people to face the facts - to understand the questions which Christianity claims to answer. And they are very terrifying facts." -CS Lewis, *Mere Christianity*.

Let me say that, without becoming religious, it is worth your time to investigate the answers presented by Christianity. That being said, I still have a lot of questions. When people ask the hard questions, I am compelled to admit that I just don't know. I don't know how things can be the way they are. I continue to ask why. I hope we never stop shouting out our questions. Someone might just be listening. In our prayers, we might just find our way.

"Why would a good God create a world like this one?" Have you caught a glimpse of what has been making its way into the very centre of my world view for thirty-some years now? From great Christian writers I have come to believe that if we were to assemble the best minds in the world with the task of creating a laboratory in which we would place human beings, with the purpose of challenging them to be better people, no environment would be more suited to the task than life itself.

We all know that the consequences of our actions are as real as any could ever be. If I fail in life, I will pay a price. If I don't play nice with my friends, I will lose them. If I break the rules and get caught, the police will come with their guns and lock me up.

Upon the premise that there is a God who set out to create our world, we conclude that this God is wisdom, not just a very wise being, but the essence of wisdom itself. If this God is also the essence of love, then He has done all of this for our benefit and for our making, to build an enduring wellness within us. If all of that is true, then we can accept that our life situation is not only the best possible world scenario. Rather, it is the only one that could accomplish what a truly good God would want, that is, Shalom: Consummate Health for Creation.

Peace. Love. Joy. Goodness. Gentleness. Kindness. Faith. The ability to put up with one another. And the desire to learn, grow, and cooperate with each other. And more. Much, much more!

To date I find no philosophy that can shake my confidence. This world with its solid, immovable laws provides the fixed, natural setting where humans can meet and interact. We are stuck in it. I am here with you and billions of like beings. We cannot escape this world or each other. I continue to breathe involuntarily. Tomorrow is coming.

We are then faced with very real questions, like, "What kind of persons will we become? Will we overcome the obstacles, pressures, and temptations of life? Or will we succumb?" No one can avoid these tests and trials.

If life, as many scientists proclaim, is just a collision of mindless energy, purposeless neutrons, and unguided nutrients, then I stand in awe of the absolute beauty that comes from the accidental formation of unfathomable worlds.

I am forced to applaud the great achievements of No One.

I will stand and praise the-emptiness-that-didn't-put-all-of-this-together. I must worship purposelessness. Because without an intelligence driving the manufacturing process there can be no purpose. If there is no purpose you have just wasted your time pondering these questions. Because there is no answer. If there is no answer, let us eat drink and be merry for tomorrow we die.

Is there no point? No purpose? No reason?

Photo by Gerry Bast, Country Road west of Calgary

Everything we have ever learned from science says that nothing happens without a cause. Nothing ever came from nothing. Nothing ever happened without something prompting it.

And in the field of language, the word "nothing" can be correct when used to explain actions. It is quite correct to say, "I did nothing." Or, "I saw nothing." However, there is nowhere you can point to and say, "That is nothing." There is no minuscule point in the universe that contains "nothing." The whole of Creation is filled with something. Even space, so-called, is filled with matter. And every "something" is built with a mysterious energy as its building block.

If I Was God . . . I would be that building block. I would be the energy that fills everything.

CHAPTER 14

—

Gerry's Turn to Meet God

Everybody has faith in something. The capitalist is playing hard at the game, hoping that he who dies with the greatest record of success wins. One type of atheist is putting his trust in a limited and biased view of science. Another is hoping that the failures of religious people and organizations are enough to throw out the Baby Jesus with the bath water. I cannot help but bank on the confidence that Someone-Out-There is tirelessly working on my behalf, building character, tearing down my selfish nature, and attempting to make me the kind of person who can love well and live well . . . forever.

If I Was God . . . I would want to be known as the giver of all good things. I would ask all people, regardless of their financial status or earning power, to learn how to trust for the provision of all of their needs. I would try to teach all people to share. I would also know that humans learn at their own speed and only when they are ready. As the maker of humanity, I would understand that education has to happen in stages. Step 2 should follow Step 1. A student will need the knowledge of Step 2 to be able to comprehend the concepts presented in Step 3.

I would be patient. If I Was God . . . I wouldn't care if it took sixty years for some people (like Gerry) to learn of my ways. Just as long as they would finally get some of it.

Therefore, If I Was God . . . I would be prepared to wait on humanity in the same way a vintner ages a fine wine.

We can learn to trust. We are beginning to share.

If I Was God . . . I would agree with Jill, who says, "If we had faith, we would be the most secure people in the world. Economies could rise and fall, and we would not be shaken."

If I Was God . . . I would agree with the writer in scripture who said, some people think that "gain is godliness. But godliness (wellness - within and in lifestyle) with contentment is great gain."

If I Was God . . . I would want to take care of everyone's financial needs (actually I would want all people to trust me to take care of all needs) so that they could enjoy life. Even if a person has more than enough, he or she can be a slave to the quest for more and more. Those who have the most often suffer with the greatest fear of losing it. Also, a person with nothing can just as easily worship and live for what they don't have.

I would tell Gerry Bast to be calm; Do Not Fear. If I Was God and Gerry was driving home with the weight of financial difficulty weighing on his mind I would have a car pull up in front of him with these letters on the licence plate EGB - I would say, "Easy, G.B." When Gerry would begin to doubt the message of comfort sent for his eyes to see, I would immediately have another car pull up beside with the letters EZY. I would say again, Easy, G.B. And if I Was God, I would laugh out loud with Gerry in his car.

If I Was God . . . and Gerry needed more assurance I would move a real estate agent to put a sign outside Gerry's bedroom window to remind him every morning that he is not alone. In very bold numbers, the agent's phone number would be the date of Gerry's birth, surrounded by 7's. I would proclaim my awareness of him.

I would give Gerry dreams in the middle of the night, declaring my overriding ability to pick up where humanity falls short.

I would nudge strangers to tell Gerry that I know where he is at, that I am with him and I am able to move him forward into my next steps for him.

If I Was God . . . I would encourage everyone to feel free to explore all that I have taught over the years. Reconsider who you think God really is. Isn't that what you would expect from the creator of a world that is anything but static? We, the Christians, have historically made the false claim that the knowledge of God is fixed in stone. We have said that all that needs to be known is already written. But humanity is always growing. Knowledge is always increasing. We are constantly evolving. Our picture of God is always changing from one great rendering to another. We are always being stretched to see deeper and to understand more.

And I would want everybody to lay down his or her selfish ambitions. Release the pressure mounting from competitive spirits. Renounce motives based on a desire to be better than somebody else. If we want to compete, we can measure ourselves against our previous efforts. Step aside. Let someone else excel. We could even lie down and let others use us as stepping stones, just like mountain goats do when they meet on a ridge and the path is too narrow for both to pass. (Is that just a myth? If so, it's a good one.)

But when Gerry Bast would show up on my doorstep, I would be happy to see him. Gerry would cry like a baby when he saw me; like a big, blubbering, broken-down, grown-up infant.

He would be thrilled to see me.

"Oh my God. Oh my God."

"That's me," I would say to Gerry, If I Was God.

"Jesus?"

"That's me."

"I'm so glad to see you."

Then Gerry would fall and kneel at my feet. And the crying . . . .

"Hey, come on. Get up. Let's sit over here."

On My Front Porch are two worn wooden rocking chairs.

"Wow! Look at the faux finish on those chairs."

"Faux finish? Nothing is an imitation here, Gerry. These are natu-rally worn through like that. Some real asses have plunked themselves down here."

"What? Asses? Ha. Yeah. I guess so, eh? Not all of them went inside with you, did they?"

"Nope."

"How could they possibly choose not to go in to that party? Seriously, listen to the laughter inside your house. It's so contagious."

"Well," I (God) would say. "People have a lot of things they are hanging on to."

"What could be more important than this?"

"You might be surprised. Have a look inside, Gerry."

Gerry would peek in the door and recognize a lot of people. "Some of these guys aren't dead. I thought this was Heaven. What are they doing here?"

"You have been to my parties a lot. You have lived a life of celebra-tion in the midst of the regular stuff of life. Did you think this was just going to suddenly become a fairy tale? Life doesn't only start when you die. I've been giving life to everyone who would seek that kind of value. Actually, I give life to everyone who asks. But everything you cling to means that you have to let go of something else. There's only so much you can keep."

Then Gerry would look at me . . . If I Was God, and Gerry would say, "Are you suggesting that I might be holding on to something?

Something else is more important than this? No way. Let's go. I have been looking for this place all of my life."

"Yes. You have, but—"

Gerry would be shocked. "But? What do you mean, but?"

I would have to break the news to Gerry, If I Was God. "You've got some things to deal with before you can go in to my house."

"Yeah. I guess I knew that was coming."

"You don't know some of it, my friend."

"Uh oh. I know that there is stuff with my family. I'm ready to apologize again. I—"

"Yeah, there is that."

"What?"

Jesus would look almost stern. "Well. Do you think that's it, Gerry?"

"Uh . . . yeah. Right. Confess. Get it out. Get forgiveness."

"You think it's that easy to 'Get it out'?"

"Uh oh."

"Uh oh, indeed. You enjoyed being the victim, didn't you? You think that all the criticism you dished out was okay because you were hurt. That doesn't fly here."

"Oh. That."

"We are just getting started, my son."

"At least you call me your son. I guess that's a good sign. At least you didn't say 'I never knew you.'"

"Everybody is my son. Except for those who are my daughters, of course."

Gerry wouldn't feel like laughing quite yet. "This is going to be difficult, isn't it?"

"Maybe."

"How long do I have to figure it out?"

"How soon do you want to get inside?"

"Uh. Like, right now."

"You don't know how they felt. But you will. They got hurt just as bad as you, and then you blamed them for your pain."

"I was the youngest. They should have helped me." Gerry's voice would kind of fade away near the end of that sentence.

"Are you gonna play that card with me? You don't know what was going on inside their heads."

"Sorry."

"Not yet, you aren't."

"Oh man. Seriously? I had no idea they were—"

"Gerry. You were too busy looking at your own pitiful self."

"Ouch!" Gerry would squirm a little.

"Ouch for them."

"Are they here?"

"Every one of them is inside."

"Really? Where is Jill?"

"Jill comes to my parties all the time. She's still back on the other side, though. Waiting her turn to make the final crossover."

"I was so hard to live with, wasn't I?"

"You were both pretty needy when you got together. There is so much opposition in the world to just being human. And even more against relationships of all kinds. But you were both pretty beat up. It was like a curse hanging over you, but at the same time, that is what drew you together. You needed each other."

"We were both so lonely before we met."

"It's not good for people to be alone. Life hurts. People cry. Some never find a soul mate to walk through it with."

"You will help her?"

"Oh yes I will! She's very hard on herself, though. She can't forgive you until she lets herself off the hook. Releasing pain and injury isn't easy for anybody. You know what? Nobody gets into my house with that crap hanging off of them. Your family had so much religion. It's creepy!" I would say that . . . If I Was God.

"I know, man. Our family."

"Most people just don't know how to live. So much beauty all around. Amazing people. Simple pleasures. So much love to be shared. Instead, humanity creates religion after religion. All of the so-called sacred exercises could bring people to an understanding of life. However, they choose the activity and miss out on the life. You too, Gerry."

"Still? I've spent years trying to let go of systems and forms of so-called holy living."

"Uh huh. Why do you sit up at night and worry? Be honest. Do you think that if you say things just right I'll forgive you? Give me a break. Do you expect to repeat words you've heard, hoping I'll go through a checklist or something? Seriously? You don't trust me. You don't know my heart. Even now you're trying to find something to say. Like I need you to grovel or something. Get over it."

"Oh man. Oh God."

"That's me, buddy."

"Right. What should I do?"

Then, very gently, I would say to Gerry, "There is nothing you 'should' do. What do you want to do?"

"I want to see my family."

"Art's on his way." At that moment, Gerry's oldest brother would step out onto the porch from inside the party with Mom and Dad in tow.

"Mom? Dad? You look just like your wedding picture! Mom, you're gorgeous! I had no idea." Gerry would lean in to his parents, and the three of them would hug. A healing pneuma of fresh air would flow deep into the trio's lungs, expanding them with each breath. Lungs would act like a pump in the atmosphere on my front porch, for drawing in love across tube-like hairs so that the ethereal oxygen could move into their hearts, pushing out fear, loneliness, self-loathing, and all harmful impurities. This air would also be free to all. Gerry would marvel at the intelligence in his father's eyes that had once been ravaged by years of dementia.

The brand new Mahlon Bast would look at his youngest son. "Gerry, I was always so proud of you and all my kids. I just had too much baggage to show it." Gerry's mind would swim with memories. "I should have . . . ." No words would follow.

An embrace. A knowing look. Another embrace.

When Gerry stepped back and turned to his brother . . . well, he would suddenly know things hidden deep inside, that no one had ever seen. And the crying would start again. Gerry is such a baby.

"I am so sorry . . . and I'm so happy to see you."

"Me too." At that point, even God couldn't remember who had said it first.

Actually, If I Was God . . . I would never be able to remember what it was that they were apologising for. Once the apology had been made, it would disintegrate and be lost forever. The two of them would hug and then sit down in the ancient chairs. Nobody would have to say much, knowing the unknowable. And then Marilyn would come out.

"Oh God." Gerry would look like a man who suddenly remembered where an object of great value had been lost. Memories and regret mingled with joy and laughter.

But there was something hanging over them, and she would speak first. "I already forgave you, Gerr. When I got here, I had to forgive and be forgiven. But then I forgot about our stuff until I saw you here just now."

"I'm so sorry. Do you remember that time I—"

"I do." She'd say, "I was so hurt. We were so close. We all had lots to forgive and forget. But I loved you so much. I forgave you a lifetime ago."

"You did?"

"Yes, I did. Since being here I've seen how difficult families and relationships are. Everybody gets hurt along the way." A moment of confusion would shadow her face, and Gerry's sister would lose her focus. "What were we talking about?" And then, "Wow." She would be visibly taken by surprise. "It is so hard to get used to that. You just apologised for something, didn't you? It happens like that every time. The instant you 'fess up to something or forgive someone, in that very moment you can't even remember what it was. Oh it is so good to see you."

"I really forgot how much I loved you, Marilyn."

"Hey there, bro. Whaaaaaat's happenin'?"

"Donald! Look at you! 1960's hippie! You look gooooood!"

Gerry would do a secret handshake with the middle brother of the family, dance a little jig, and Don would start to speak, but Gerry would jump in. "We used to argue."

"Yeah. We sure did," Don would agree. "You were so stubborn."

"You needed me to be stubborn. Damn, I wanted to kick your ass. Excuse the language."

Jesus (actually me, If I Was God) quietly watching the parade, would speak up, "Nothing gets excused here. It has all been paid for. But then, everybody takes out their own garbage. And by the way, I would love to kick some butts too. But all I have to do is sit them down on those chairs, and their own consciences take care of the kicking."

Gerry would turn back to Don. "I said some pretty harsh stuff."

"We have a lot to talk about, Gerr. We got messed up, and I thought I had it all figured out. But who could have known what God has in store for those who love Him?"

Gerry would look around at his brothers and sister. "How many times did I . . . ." Suddenly, the answer to his own question. "Really? I am so sorry."

Art would speak. "Life took some crazy turns. We needed room to breathe. Then we all took it out on each other. It's a common disease. But let me tell you, there is no confusion here. We know precisely in what way and how much you got hurt. We have also seen clearly your intentions, and we understand where you were coming from. We have the freedom to forgive."

Marilyn would conclude the matter by saying, "We have had the time to let go of our petty claims. To use a worn-out phrase, it's all good. It is all so very good. It is finished."

At this point, Jesus would step into the circle of conversation. "I've got someone I'd like you to meet, Gerry." And at that, a forty-something, very wise yet youthful male would step out onto the porch.

With no possible means of knowing this ancient Hebrew rabbi, Gerry somehow would. "It is so great to meet you. Oh my God!"

"No. I am not your God. I am just an old rabbi."

"You are definitely not old. You look so . . . so alive!" Gerry would be clearly in shock at the youthful presence before me.

"Thanks. I feel just fine since making the journey here two thousand and some years ago . . . in your time, that is."

"Rabbi Johakim! First century Johakim! You feel pretty good? Wow! I guess you would."

The rabbi would turn to Gerry's parents, who were taking it all in, and ask, "Is this your other son?"

"Yes. He's the baby of the family." (I can tell you honestly, my mom never stopped saying that until the day she died. I can imagine Norma is still telling everyone she meets that I'm the baby. By the way, I'm doing everything in my power to live up to it.)

"Hey Joe," Jesus would say to Johakim, "I'd like you to take a few minutes with Gerry. He's had some issues, shall we say. But he'd really like to come to the party."

"As you wish." After chatting about my history and getting to know me a little, the former contemporary of Jesus would gesture towards the stairs.

Down onto the lawn that was a little unkempt, Gerry would be reminded of his grandfather's farm. The machinery, the buildings, and the cattle were of first priority, but the length of the grass at the homestead where we used to go for summer holidays, was not. At this house there are higher priorities than grooming the lawn also.

"Listen, Gerry, there's a touch of chutzpah in even the best men and women. But when we get honest, we clearly see the paradox within our own hearts. We believe and we doubt, we hope and get depressed, we love and we despise our neighbours. Then we can't even allow ourselves to feel good. I used to feel bad because I wasn't feeling guilty. We're all meshugener!"

"I'm not sure why, but somehow I know what you mean. Chutzpah is arrogance, and meshegas is insane. Isn't that Yiddish?"

"Yes it is. Way more fun than Aramaic."

"More fun than Aramaic. That's hilarious! Ouch! We are meshugener! What the heck is wrong with us?"

"It doesn't mean we're in any more tsuris (serious trouble) than the next guy, but we have been on a journey. We are kind of like a group of people on an eleven day road trip who get side-tracked, and it takes decades to reach their destination."

Gerry would remember a story about a man named Moses on a trip through the desert and ponder out loud. "Forty years of wandering for what could have taken less than two weeks. I guess they had some things to learn."

Rabbi Johakim: "Have you ever noticed that when you finally get serious about living well and finding harmony, you're still playing games? You decide to give some time to help someone else, and suddenly you're so proud of yourself for helping out, you can't do it for them anymore. It becomes your shtick, something you do, trying to get some points when you only look like a mentsh. Nobody is that good. It's hard for an old Jewish boy to live by grace, to live in the understanding that everything is already provided for us. It goes against all things thought to be most human, like being in control, for example. You have to be ready to let go. Don't be holding on to your tenure as a good man, as a great Christian. Christianity is a strange concept." And then Johakim would turn and look as though he was gazing back into the past.

"As if Jesus wanted to start a religion and have it named after himself. You have no idea how meshugena that sounds to me, having known him, having watched him live and die. Jesus starting a new religion! Now that's funny!"

Laughing, the old-man-made-young-again would begin to lose control, holding on to his well-rounded belly. Seeing his tears would leave Gerry wondering whether sadness was welling up. Seeing it through his eyes, the strongholds of religion, the tangents taken, and the damage done to the life taught by the master, he too would be overwhelmed. Finally, they would have to reach down to sit on the ground and catch their breath.

"Then the rabbi would begin to speak from his ever-expanding wisdom. "There are many deities being created on planet Earth.

Promises are made that can never be kept. But the God I know, the One who designed the universe; the Creator of suns and stars and planets and energy and every minute detail holding it all together, the mastermind that could speak humanity into existence, that God doesn't need anyone to vouch for Him.

That God had the intelligence, actually, that God is the intelligence that maintains and continues to create new worlds as we speak. Did you know that the colour of space is different on the outer edge of the ever forming universe? It is! The matter that fills space is kind of pink when it is brand new! You will have to see it for yourself. His creativity continues to design worlds. Everything created is breathtaking when you begin to understand the magnitude of design built into every speck.

"The absolute genius who designed you is not surprised by your actions, even when you shock yourself by failing to live up to your own expectations. When you watch the world from this vantage point and see the things that humanity does, you realize that Yahweh has the greatest sense of humour. That's right! He smiles like a father watching toddlers trying to do a puzzle. Yet people will answer for the bupkes they have caused. (Once meant to depict actions or things considered worse than useless – ie. goat droppings.) And patience! He really believes in us. God knows that His design will fulfill His purpose. It took ages for me to understand that. But I finally do. We will all learn who we are and what Jeshua's influence on humanity really means.

"So Gerry, you are just about ready to get over the whole guilt and anguish scenario. And . . . you may have the power to believe where others deny, to hope where others despair, to love where others refuse. But that ability is sheer gift; it is not a reward for your faith or for praying. Even our faithfulness is a gift."

Silence. A deep and quiet pause. Then, rising to their feet again without saying another word, they would walk back.

"Listen." Johakim would get very serious after they were back on the porch. "It feels like it's going to kill us when we allow the emotional surgery to cut deep into the stuff we hold so dear. Don't resist." And with that, he would head back inside. A wave and a sincere, "I'll see you soon."

Back on the front porch, more work would be necessary to rid Gerry of the dis-ease in his soul. Memories would flash like a crystal-clear HD screen, and suddenly Gerry's thoughts would feel like they were made of real matter: sharp, slicing edges.

Other scenes would play out in his mind. People who had encountered his selfish, whiny-ass, pity-party criticism would suddenly be standing right there on that porch . . . so much pain. So many people. Images and faces playing out before him. Working through . . . negotiating, bargaining, anger, grief, denial, back to bargaining . . . how long it would seem to take! Then finally acceptance and peace.

Gerry would turn to Jesus and ask, "Is this my judgement?"

"Yes it is. But let me tell you, everything I do is for a reason. And that reason is never to just punish someone. Never! I want to flush it all out until you are truly free."

"That's what my brother Don always said."

Then Jesus would get as gentle as anyone could be, "You've got some things you're not letting go of yet, Gerry. Some people need to hear that you aren't going to keep a record on them. You've been hurt, and I'd like you to give up the anger still brewing inside."

Memories on the screen of Gerry's mind again, slashing against his skin. Stabbing deep into his flesh. The weight of them pressing on his heart like a car lying across one's chest. And under the crush, grasping his stomach . . . blood-covered hands. "Am I actually bleeding?"

Then, seeing the tears in Jesus' eyes, noticing Jesus' blood-soaked hands and side, "This is your blood, isn't it? I'm so sorry. I am so, so sorry."

Jesus would look at Gerry with all-knowing eyes, "I know. I knew it all along. It has all been taken care of. Nothing gets swept under a rug here. It is dealt with. You don't have to do anything. I paid your debt. This whole exercise was for your healing; to set you free. Your heart is soft." A long pause. "You know that we weren't holding anything against you, don't you? Everybody needs to deal with their own hang-ups."

"This was all for me? You weren't angry?"

"You have no idea how much we want to be with you and with every single person. All of this was put together so that we could be family. The whole of Creation is a home that we built for you. There is no agenda except loving, healthy community, and you're it, buddy. Humanity. Friends. Family."

And then, there it would be; rather, there they would be. Thousands of people approaching the front porch. Some plunking their butts down on those old wooden chairs. Others sneaking a preview of the party going on inside. It seemed as though there were only a few crowding onto the steps, but if you looked closely and could concentrate on something other than Jesus, you would see that the length of the porch now spread out in both directions. For just a split second, a flash of supernatural sight, you could see the railing and the stairs and people and Jesus, the whole scenario stretching out and curving with the horizon of the new Earth. There was literally no end and no beginning. It was a new dimension. Physics would never explain this. The Front Porch appeared to encircle the planet. And at the same time – I, Gerry, know it's not possible in our limited perception of three dimensions – but I swear I could also see the floor boards, the railing with the two wooden chairs making a 90 degree turn around the house and heading north, over and over and over again. People everywhere.

And somehow I knew that they all hadn't died and were coming to meet the judge, as it were. They were all there in whatever state they happened to be at that moment. Kids in high school. Aging grandparents. Many long dead and returning to the porch to find themselves, to reclaim their humanity. All walks of life. All persuasions. Happy, angry, sad, disillusioned, religious, spiritual, gay and straight, dead and alive. Every single person trying to get into the party or denying there even was a party, and others trying every which way possible to be accepted or debating what the party was all about and who could get into the party, or shouting about how exclusive the party was, or arguing against someone who had already entered through that door. Every single person making their own choice.

There was a set of stairs every few feet. On every single stair stood a person or two. Others were out on the lawn. Some people appeared to be hiding their faces, staring at the ground or leaning against the tree. And if you could concentrate for just a little longer, your eyes would grasp the reality that beside every single one of them, Jesus also stood, giving them his undivided attention. Even those who couldn't face him. Maybe especially those. The Creator-with-great-earnest-for-all was with each one.

And suddenly I didn't just see it. I felt it. The air wrapped around me with limitless, unbounded compassion. The eyes of Jesus looking intently at every one of us. Delving into every corner of every single thought of each and every person. Calling all of us out of our fear. Drawing us away from the very things that had enslaved us our whole lives. Compassion. Absolute, undivided attendance to all persons, regardless of their status. Pure, uninhibited love. It was emotional, spiritual, intellectual, and even physical. It was far above erotic. Every cell within my body, every thought, every feeling was brought to the limits of ecstasy. There was nothing sexual about it, but, I wondered, if sex could have been this good, humanity would never have survived as long as we did. No one would ever have bothered to eat. Why would you? This enveloping atmosphere satisfied every need and brought a person to the point where it truly hurt to take any more in. And then . . . I wanted more.

I fell to my knees under the weight of crushing love. I wept like a baby. I shook uncontrollably and he touched me and I stood on my feet and stared deeply into his eyes.

My heart beat full and strong. I could feel my veins flowing with the happiness I had never imagined was possible. Every muscle in my body suddenly felt alive. I felt as though I could run as fast as I wanted. I could jump anywhere, lift anything and carry it with ease for as long as I chose. My mind suddenly knew as well as I had been known by God. If I wanted to be somewhere, I could think myself there. If I wanted to be with someone, I would be able to be with them just by willing it. However, I was with Him. I didn't want anything else.

He had started everything. Jesus had completed all. I was whole.

"Can I show you your treasures?" he asked.

"I have treasures?"

"Oh yeah. You sure do. You have invested well, Gerry."

"I find that hard to believe."

Then Jesus showed me, Gerry, all the people I had spent time with, everyone I had loved. Even my inability to love people was rewarded for my failed attempts. They were attempts, after all. Every time I had given one second of my attention when it wasn't convenient for me had been deposited into some kind of account and had been gathering a compound interest. When anyone had carried away a sense of value from an encounter with me and then, in turn, had shared that appreciation with another person, I received interest on that deposit also. I realized that I was also being rewarded for just breathing in all the life I had been given.

The two of us walked away from the porch and down to a stream. The Creator of all things sat with me and watched the water meander past in hyper HD. We stayed there for what seemed like an eternity without saying a word as my mind opened up to the reality that all things had worked together for my good.

Jesus finally broke the silence. "I love rivers and streams. Water was such a great idea. It is an absolute miracle what water does for a planet." He seemed to be very proud of his invention.

Then we talked for another couple of eons about the Earth and about people and how it had cost so much to put all of this together. At that moment I was so glad that he had chosen to go through with his plans to create humanity. Life was so worth all that I had been through. And I knew that it would be for every living being as we let go of our egos. We were being asked by the One who knew us all to let go and let life do its work in us. Breathe. Take it in. Take all of it.

Jesus got up and said, "Soon it will be time for you to get to work. My kingdom stretches throughout the ever-expanding universe, and I want to show you where you are needed most."

Then, finally, the words that I, Gerald Edwin Bast, had been waiting for my whole life were spoken by Jesus himself. "But before you go to work, Gerry, I know where there is a great party going on. Do you want to check it out?"

ONE FINAL NOTE

I Would Become One of Us

The success of Alcoholics Anonymous can be largely accredited to their mantra in reply to every broken person . . . "Me too."

If I Was God . . . I would become a human and live among my people, just once, so that I could feel what they feel.

I would learn what it meant to fear what they fear and to hurt the way they hurt.

I would laugh with them,

Cry when they cry,

Run out of energy in the same way they collapse from exhaustion.

I would love them as they learn how to love each other,

And I would bleed just like all people bleed.

If I Was God . . . I would be their neighbour.

And I would show them that they are my people,

My family,

My most beloved friends.

If I Was God . . . I would weep with sisters who have lost their brother to disease.

I would stay awake all night praying that they would somehow come to understand,

That I had come so that they might have life – full, invigorating life.

If I Was God . . . I would live and die,

Just like they all live and expire.

I would live and die to show them that the life I gave them was worth the risk.

I would help them see that they were worth the risk.

And then . . . If I Was God . . . I would not stay dead.

Because I AM LIFE and

Life does not die.

Life, by its very definition, does not die.

In the same way that darkness cannot expel light . . .

In that same way,

Death does not have the final say.

I would die, just like all people die.

But I could not possibly stay dead.

Death could not hold me.

Because I Am . . .

I Am! I don't just exist, I Am.

And those to whom I have given life,

Because I have lived,

And died,

And have lived again ...

They shall live also.

Because Life cannot die . . .

And because I conquered death . . .

My friends will live also. That's what I would do ... If I Was God.

IF I WAS GOD, THE SONG

—

by Gerry Bast

You have come to the end of my humble offering. These are only a sampling of the things any person could encounter on the journey to knowledge – the most valuable knowledge – knowing one's self, one's environment, and one's Creator. Perhaps the most important statement of all is this . . . If I Was God . . . I would be proud to have made you.

You may quickly find the reading of lyrics quite boring. If so, don't be afraid to put the book down and call it done. Thank you so much for allowing me to add to your thoughts on such important topics. I invite you to join the conversation.

If you can find the cadence of the lyrics below, I will be thrilled. I place it here for musicians with the hope that the right person will see this and want to work with it. Thanks for taking the time to hear for yourself what I would do If I Was God. May the real God bless you and all you hold dear. Amen.

For song updates and to view all photos in full color please go to www.ifiwasgod.ca - Note: DO NOT USE .COM

If I Was God.

If I Was God and could form a world,

Would I build a home
Like the Earth we know and live in?

If I Was God, with a heart for love,
Would I be bold?
Would I breathe life into children?

If I Was God, would I make you?
Would I take the chance and
Risk my heart on your decision?

Chorus

If I Am . . . the Original Thought
If I Am . . . the First Creative Idea
If I Am . . . If I Am.
Then what will I do?

If I have the Original Heart.
If I have the Power to Build.
Then I will. I think I will.
I'll create a home for you.

I could play it safe.
I could make more stars and planets.
What if we just had animals?
Imagine a world without all the bickering humans.
How beautiful would planet Earth be if there were no people
        polluting.
How great would this blue marble be if there was no one fighting wars.
What if we had never clear-cut a forest, had never destroyed a species?
Let your mind picture a world without people.

If I Was God I could shape the stars.
And design this world
To explode with life and energy.

If I Was God and could make you
If I could give you life
And invest in your reality.

If I Was God I could fill this world
With the hope for peace
And build a love community.

If I Am . . . the Original One
If I Am . . . the Mother of All
If I Am . . . If I Am.
Will I imagine you?

If I have the Original Spark.
If I have the Seed of Life
Then I will. Yes I will.
I will give birth to you.

But wait. Would I lay it all on the line?
Could I face your rejection?
If I started all of this and it all went the way it has.
Would I be appreciated?
Would you really want to thank me for all of this?

What's the point? Is there some kind of purpose behind all of this?
Sometimes it feels like an experiment gone wrong.
Was it worth the risk?
People hoarding.
Others are starving.
Self-ish. Not giving.
Self-ish. Not sharing.
Self-ish. Not generous.

If I had made the Original Man
If I'd created that First Girl
Would I smile? Would I smile?

At the very thought of you?

If I had heard that first heartbeat.
And had felt your pain all along.
Would I try? Would I try?
To come and rescue you?

God did make the Original Man.
God did build the Magnificent Girl.
God does smile. God does smile.
And God would do it again.

ACKNOWLEDGEMENTS, SUGGESTED READING AND QUOTATIONS WITHIN *IF I WAS GOD*

——

I continue to provide my wife, Jill, with tests of patience. One of which was the undertaking to write this book. She stays with me and is still passing those tests! Much love.

Many thanks to our favourite daughter-in-law Amy Asbury and Asbury Studios for work on the photos inside these covers: www.amyasbury.ca

Now it is time to talk about the writers who have influenced me and offer some suggestions for your journey towards greater understanding and a more hopeful worldview.

Much effort has been made to obtain permission for works quoted or photos used. If proper acknowledgements have been omitted, or any rights overlooked, it is unintentional. Please notify the publisher if you discover any such mistake and it will be corrected in future editions. The following authors have been of great consequence in my life. At times I have quoted them in the chapters you have read. Credit is due them for providing a broad foundation for not only living life but also for thriving in the midst of reality. There was no ticket to Easy Street, no set of instructions, and no step by step procedures guaranteeing success. I owe a debt of gratitude to these people for opening my heart and for giving me the confidence to question the status quo.

CS Lewis captured our hearts and jumpstarted our ability to think beyond the obvious.

Rob Bell, along with many others, now leads a generation into new thought and believable hope. With him, many voices are calling us to Join the Conversation and accept our responsibility in the task of Repainting the Christian Faith for our generation.

VELVET ELVIS – Repainting the Christian Faith by Rob Bell © copyright 2005 Zondervan, Grand Rapids, Michigan. (Now available through Harper Collins Publishers)

WHAT WE TALK ABOUT WHEN WE TALK ABOUT GOD by Rob Bell is a book of great genius. We are living in a time of change and God is not being left behind. He has been pulling us forward throughout history at moments of Divine Intervention. You are living in one of those extraordinary seasons of change.

LOVE WINS, A Book About Heaven, Hell, and the Fate of Every Person Who Ever Lived by Rob Bell.

THE SHACK - by Wm. Paul Young is a fictional, global bestseller that will take you on most valuable, but wild journey. Take that journey! Do it as soon as you can!

MERE CHRISTIANITY by CS Lewis © copyright CS Lewis Pte Ltd 1942, 1943, 1944, 1952.

Quotations in *If I Was God*, from MERE CHRISTIANITY. Used by Permission.

A long, long time ago THE GREAT DIVORCE by CS Lewis challenged me to question the accepted ideas regarding judgement and the whole heaven/hell scenario.

SOUL SURVIVOR - How My Faith Survived the Church by Philip Yancey. Yancey is brutally honest about faith and doubt, along with the imperfect humans leading our churches. No criticism. No judgemental finger pointing and no cover up.

WHAT'S SO AMAZING ABOUT GRACE by Philip Yancey

BLUE LIKE JAZZ by Donald Miller. Wow! Get it. Read it. Love it!

SEARCHING FOR GOD KNOWS WHAT by Donald Miller

BEAUTIFUL OUTLAW by John Eldredge. Jesus, like you've never seen him before.

KINGDOM, GRACE, JUDGMENT – Paradox, Outrage, and Vindication in the Parables of Jesus. Outside the box!!!!!

THE GREAT EMERGENCE – How Christianity is Changing and Why - by Phyllis Tickle will give you a historically based picture of the world you are now inhabiting.

THE END OF RELIGION – Encountering the Subversive Spirituality of Jesus by Bruxy Cavey © copyright NAVPRESS, Colorado Springs CO. www.navpress.com

REPENTING OF RELIGION – Turning from Judgment to the Love of God by Gregory A. Boyd. This book would win the prize for the best title ever if it weren't for . . .

EVERYTHING MUST CHANGE by Brian McLaren. How intriguing is that?

THE MEANING OF FAITH by Harry Emerson Fosdick © copyright 1917 Abingdon Press. One of the greatest Christian thinkers of the twentieth century. Also outside the box in his own right.

Quotations in If I Was God – Used by Permission

ORTHODOXY by G K Chesterton

Videos by Rob Bell

The foresight demonstrated in the video by Rob Bell entitled **THE GODS AREN'T ANGRY** is unprecedented. Allow the overriding worldview bound up in this presentation to move you into a peaceful anticipation of the future. Get it at http://www.robbell.com

The rights to use the photos in *If I Was God* have been purchased or are used by permission or are photos taken by Jill or Gerry Bast.

CPSIA information can be obtained at www.ICGtesting.com
Printed in the USA
LVOW04s1255200915

454917LV00013B/80/P

9 781460 221266